Copyright 2011 by Amy Wood, Psy.D.

Cover concept by Beth Harris-Hess
Cover and book design by Daniel Yeager, New Image Design
Nu-Images.com

Amy Wood, Psy.D.
amywoodpsyd.com

Printed in the United States of America
Modern Sage Press

First printing: January 2011

ISBN 978-0-615-42076-9

{ life your way }

REFRESH YOUR APPROACH TO SUCCESS AND BREATHE EASIER IN A FAST-PACED WORLD

By Amy Wood, Psy.D.

{ praise }
for Amy Wood's Life Your Way

"Reading *Life Your Way* is like indulging in a restorative cup of coffee with a favorite mentor. Delivered in a commonsensible, clear, and concise style, Dr. Wood's matter of fact wisdom will transport you away from the pressures of your everyday life and into a place of greater clarity, direction, and self-appreciation. By the time you finish this immensely enjoyable book, you will feel enlightened and uplifted, with an assured sense of who you are and what's important to you. You'll have a perspective that will let you simultaneously carry out your inner wisdom and deal head-on with the real, unrelenting world."

— Anne Milford,
Co-author of *How Not to Marry the Wrong Guy*

"*Life Your Way* provides an original approach to the problems that plague most of us: overwhelming information and demands. Wood offers practical ideas to refashion your process for work and life and then urges you to take the steering wheel. Few books go beyond 'pump you up' rhetoric, but this one is packed with powerful examples and clear advice, making navigating the overwhelm possible."

— Jennifer Comeau, President, I-Amplitude
Consulting and Coaching

"Dr. Wood offers an engaging, thoughtful, and page-turning book with plenty of examples from her many clients and from her own life experiences to help readers develop a realistic plan for a more satisfying life. Each chapter ends with practical homework assignments to move the reader in a more productive direction. Her book both instructs and motivates and is likely to be a helpful resource for many."

— **Thomas Plante, Ph.D.,**
Author of *Spiritual Practices in Psychotherapy*,
Blogger for *Psychology Today*

"Amy gets to the heart of the matter in true-to-life scenarios we can relate to. Whether it's shaking up our career, valuing innate abilities we might take for granted, or understanding what's really behind a desire for a new job, we can benefit from Amy's no-nonsense approach to situations that keep us stuck."

— **Barbara Babkirk,** Founder
Heart At Work Career Counseling

"Reading Life Your Way is like sitting in a chair next to Dr. Wood and having her talk to you like a friend, mentor and psychologist, all in one. Develop a relationship with your intuition and you will find success on your own terms is her core message and it is delivered in a captivating, conversational manner interlaced with stories from her own life and from those of her clients. In a world overloaded with self-help books, as she candidly points out, Life Your Way is unique in that it tells us we have all the self-help we need already, in our intuition, if we just take the time to cultivate it. Dr. Wood gives us a new "blueprint" on how to do that with exercises and ways to "Apply the Wisdom." Life Your Way is a practical, grounded, and inspiring book that offers the perfect prescription to cure our overwhelmed and overbusy lives."

— **Susanna Liller,** Author of *Circle Power*

"Life Your Way is a delightful and thought-provoking book. Dr. Wood makes her message—that all of us have what we already need to make the changes we desire (or not) in life—very accessible through her highly engaging writing style. The "Apply the Wisdom" part of each chapter allows readers to consider the advice they have just read and apply it as they wish to their own personal situations. I see this being a popular title for any public library to own."

— **Stephanie Limmer,**
Director, Kennebunk (Maine) Free Library

"You can't force focus- it's a process of letting go; turning off the noise. Amy Wood has crafted a powerful guide to help you focus on what's important and let go of what simply isn't working. This is not another pop-psych "5 simple steps" manual; it's a well designed process for developing a clear picture of your life and rationally sorting out your goals and ambitions on your own terms.

The word "meaningful" appears throughout Life Your Way. You can do personal development busy work, or you can attack self-improvement in a substantive and meaningful way. Amy Wood has provided you with a meaningful way to improve yourself- you supply the meaning!"

— **Jim Bouchard**, Author of *Think Like a Black Belt*

"Life Your Way is smart, accessible, and fun to read – and it offers advice that actually works in the real world."

— **Jeff Fisher,** Writer/Director, *Killer Movie*

"Dr. Amy Wood has written a modern self-help book with a fresh approach to revitalizing adult anxiety. Rather than relying on cliché gender stereotypes, she respectfully speaks to her audience like complex people who have diverse needs and unique developmental paths. Her message targets the hyper fast-food culture we live in and offers an antidote of balance, slowing down, being thoughtful, knowing oneself, and taking control, rather than seeking to be more and do more in order to adapt.

The book contains client cases, relatable anecdotes, and personal stories and reflections that are genuine, unpretentious, self-reflective, and honest. In addition, each chapter ends with challenging and fun exercises to help practice the chapter themes. The author includes many concepts in psychology throughout the text (existential anxiety, reinforcement strategies, cognitive distortions, etc.) that can be understood by any audience with or without a background in the field.

The book is written with a sort of "folk wisdom style" which is neither pretentious nor dumbed-down. She presents as a kind-of "expert anti-expert" who both recognizes the strengths of expert advice and the weaknesses of over-relying on the barrage of information that exists intended to empower us. Not surprisingly, her style in this regard seems to mimic the message she intends audiences to grasp.

All in all, I found this to be a refreshing read for those who are re-examining their lives and looking for the support and wisdom to slow down, find meaning, and both appreciate and challenge what the modern world has to offer."

— **Jack S. Kahn,** Ph.D.,
    Author of *An Introduction to Masculinities*

"*Life Your Way is like a cool glass of water on a hot day. It sustains and satisfies.*"

— **Mary Preuss Olson,** Founder and Director,
    The Magnificent Living Institute

"Dr. Wood is as engaging, down-to-earth, and stimulating from the page as she is when she speaks in front of an audience. Her calm, affirming, and very wise voice is easy to hear as you read, and her guidance is inspiring, motivating, and refreshingly to the point. No matter where you are in life or where you want to go, Dr. Wood makes you feel confident that you can make the personal and professional changes you desire."

— **Julia Kirby**, Development Director,
St. Lawrence Arts Center

"Life Your Way offers a compelling approach on how to manage the constant "Go, Do, Be Better" stresses inherent with living in the 21st century. Rather than offering strategies that deplete our "inner strength" by offering formulaic advice, Dr. Wood's approach is to guide us to use our intuition and inner knowing as critical tools to help us find the balance and confidence to restructure how we manage the hectic, busy aspects of life. By focusing on our strengths and encouraging the use of our innate wisdom and intuition, Dr. Wood provides us with key ideas and reflective exercises that will guide us to find our own balance and harmony."

—**Jeanne Whynot-Vickers**, Director of
Educational Excellence, Learning Works

"Amy Wood has written a new and improved addition to the self-help genre because she has had the confidence to see and to understand that expert advice doesn't help if it doesn't show us how we can move forward in ways that are our own. Your Way, as her title says, is what you want to improve, as her fresh and encouraging argument leads her reader to understand. Life Your Way is found in a respectful reliance on your own values, preferences, and desires at every step of any course you want to follow. She uses the strong imagery of personal intuition, self-guidance of an intimate and confident kind. Her book goes step-by-step through exercises and reflections that are reliable because they rest on what is already yours. She does not beguile with ideas of growth that would require you to live by the standards of anyone

else, or distract with promises of rewards and prizes you wouldn't want to own.

Finally, this is a friendly book written by a knowledgeable psychologist who has a gift for writing about the lessons of life, and offers what she has learned as a gift to others. Her warmth and encouragement shine through, with a steady confidence that you will be able to make good use of it to continue your growth Your Way. I heartily recommend this book, and I confidently expect you to enjoy it and benefit from reading it."

> — **Robert L. Powers**, Retired Distinguished Service Professor, Adler School of Professional Psychology

"Down to earth, wise, charming and, above all, chock full of uncommon common sense."

> — **George Vaillant,** MD, Author of *Aging Well;* Director of the Harvard Study of Adult Development

life { your } way

REFRESH YOUR APPROACH TO SUCCESS AND BREATHE EASIER IN A FAST-PACED WORLD

By Amy Wood, Psy.D.

Modern Sage Press

To know what you prefer, instead of humbly saying Amen to what the world tells you you ought to prefer, is to have kept your soul alive.

Robert Lewis Stevenson

For Richard M. Wood,

my father, who taught me the art of living well.

{ author's note }

The instructions and advice in *Life Your Way* are not intended as a substitute for psychotherapy or coaching. I disclaim any responsibility or liability resulting from actions advocated or discussed in this book.

In the interest of preserving confidentiality, the clients and circumstances portrayed in this book are composite in nature. Any resemblance of a composite character to an actual person is entirely coincidental. Stories from my personal life are true, and I have changed most names to protect privacy.

{ table of contents }

{ preamble }

Susan is an ambitious 43-year-old executive at a nonprofit agency she truly believes in. Always looking for ways she can be more effective personally and professionally, she spent $400 on self-help books and attended a weeklong intensive holistic living course and six motivational workshops last year. She receives daily blog posts and tweets from two famous life coaches and watches a week's worth of taped *Dr. Phil* shows every weekend to stay on top of new ways to achieve her full potential.

Though she can articulate all sorts of popular theories on what it takes to be content, Susan is unclear about her own goals and dreams, and longs for that one recipe for happiness that will bring her peace of mind. Every time she enthusiastically finishes a self-help book, she thinks, "This is it. If I follow these ten steps, these five principles, this new philosophy, I'll like myself and my life." But then, a few weeks later, the novelty has worn off, and she's on her way to the next book, the right book, the one that will really make the difference.

Dan, a 50-year-old married consultant, launched his own business two years ago so that he could work his schedule around taking his ailing widower father to his various doctor appointments. He regularly listens to podcasts and attends webinars on such topics as attracting customers, building wealth, closing deals, and managing time. Curious, creative, and industrious, he is constantly jumping on new ideas for growing his business. He loves brainstorming possibilities with a stream of contacts he meets through social networking sites like Facebook and LinkedIn and as a member of several professional associations.

Dan never feels finished at the end of the day despite his hard work, and his wife is often angry with him for being on his Blackberry or cell phone at home. He lies awake at night wondering how he will ever flesh out all his ideas in a way that will actually make the kind of money he needs for retirement. He is overweight and has high blood pressure. His doctor has told him a few times that he needs to eat better and lose weight. Once a star high school athlete, Dan gets what his doctor is saying but can't seem to stick to a weight-loss program.

Then there's Cathy, a 38-year-old social worker and stepmother, who prides herself on helping her clients to nurture relationships, maintain life balance, and handle pressure. She subscribes to three magazines and watches four TV shows for tips on cooking healthful food, maintaining a beautiful home, staying in good shape, and keeping her family life solid. She volunteers for three organizations and has a long list of hobbies she'd like to take up, home improvement projects she wants to tackle, and progressive ways she hopes to keep her home and community "green" and "local." Her mother died three months ago, and she attends a support group and takes an antidepressant to keep going as she works through her grief.

Once considered extremely organized and reliable, Cathy now finds herself forgetting to return emails and phone calls, not following through with promises to her stepchildren, and running late for just about everything. No matter how often she reorganizes her schedule, she can't seem to find the time or energy to fit in what she knows she needs to do to keep her life thriving: get to the gym, keep the house decluttered, catch up with her professional journals, have fun with her close friends, nurture herself, eat organically, the list goes on. Like Susan and Dan, Cathy never feels like she's doing enough. A true sense of competence and completeness is always just out of reach.

So how can this be?

How can three seemingly intelligent, directed, conscientious adults be so far from fulfillment when they are always striving to be successful at home and work? How is it that the strong sense of commitment and responsibility that used to bring about satisfaction now seems to lead only to stress?

Like many frustrated and worn-out adults today, Susan, Dan, and Cathy feel they're not getting anywhere because they're trying to advance in life with an outmoded approach. They were raised to believe that if you had the appropriate knowledge on any subject, you could apply that knowledge to move up and on in the world. Having trouble with your kids, your health, your finances, your relationships, your career, or any other adult issue? Just seek out the right professional or publication, carry out some sensible tips, experience relief and growth, and go on living your life until the next challenge arises. What you learned from school, the media, and mentors would help you to get to a better place every time.

While that open-minded, information-gathering approach made perfect sense when sources could be limited to a couple of classic self-help books and a trusted professional or adviser, it is ineffective in an age where data on how to improve our homes, families, relationships, health, personalities, bodies, self-images, careers, and communities comes at us in a relentless, rushing torrent. Constantly bombarded with ever-changing personal and professional improvement advice through books, blogs, ezines, podcasts, magazines, social networking sites, talk and news shows, email, chat rooms, websites, tweets, texts, workshops, seminars, telecourses, and webinairs, we are left with the impression that there is always some area of life that needs our attention, always a new way to do something better, always a need to be on the alert for updates. So much emphasis is put on staying aware of new trends, topics, discoveries and remedies that the need for information is constant, and our sense of personal mastery ever elusive.

In this era of information overwhelm, staying open to new solutions to problems at home and work is no longer the issue. The key to adult growth and development is upgrading our capacity for coping with and capitalizing on a flow that is only going to become more frenzied and pervasive as technology advances. We can't prevent the flow from gaining ground and force, but we can restructure and refine our existing strengths to better navigate and benefit from the onslaught. By establishing new strategies for success, strategies that draw out and fortify inner resources to calm the storm, we responsible adults can learn how to be in control, competent, confident, and complete—no matter how persuasive and persistent those professional and personal improvement appeals and antidotes become.

This book will show you how to rediscover and build on the foundation you already have within you to rise above the challenge of feeling adept and adequate in a culture where inducement to grow and develop never seems to cease. I've filled each chapter with success stories from my psychotherapy and coaching practice and my own life so that you can see from straightforward and practical examples that my suggestions really work.

Each chapter concludes with a section called *Apply the Wisdom*—manageable ways to start incorporating the lessons you learn into a new foundation for success. I encourage you to try the suggestions that appeal to you—in your own time frame, at your own pace—through writing, thinking, or conversing. Reading is insightful, but you'll see as you advance through this book that experimenting with new ideas in the real world is the most powerful way to refashion your process for personal and professional satisfaction.

{ introduction }

Boston is one of my favorite places because it has all the hallmarks of a stand-out American city: exquisite architecture, fine food, diverse neighborhoods, fabulous theater, rich history, world-class shopping, and, according to my husband, the best major league baseball team. The one thing I don't like about Boston is that it's hard to get to all those things that make the city so great—simply because the street system, established in the 18th century to accommodate horses, wagons and other transportation vehicles of that time, is now perfectly charming but antiquated. A grid that once beautifully handled city traffic patterns is perpetually jammed up because there's just not enough room for all the cars.

This is sort of what has happened to the brains of those of us who entered adulthood before the explosion of information that now overwhelms us. Once perfectly equipped to orchestrate success-oriented thinking and behavior, our adult brains now short-circuit in the face of demands that outweigh what they bargained for when they emerged in adolescence.

If you came of age in the seventies when I did, your training ground for discernment, determination, and other critical aspects of self-actualization would be considered a walk in the park by today's standards. You likely cut your smart decision-making teeth on dilemmas like choosing a favorite TV show from just three major networks, narrowing down which records you wanted to buy from Casey Kasem's weekly top 40 countdown, and selecting a college from brochures that trickled in by mail after your SATs. You acquired the art of sustained concentration by persevering through term papers and study sessions no matter how loud the music on your brother's stereo or the latest mad crush in your head. You took your personal improvement leads from a handful of inspiring teachers, relatives, coaches, and blockbuster celebrities, and you determined post–high school aspirations by considering the academic subjects for which you had an affinity.

If you were especially ambitious and curious as a pre-information age teenager, you had to put real effort into uncovering growth opportunities beyond mainstream offerings by doing library research, exploring alternative book and record shops, watching independent films at art houses, and conversing with whatever free-thinking adults came into your life. Incentives to evolve beyond the standard self-actualization milestones and rites of passage laid out by your parents, teachers, and predictable Hollywood movies came in the form of the occasional pop psychology titles— remember *I'm Okay—You're Okay* and *Games People Play?*— that caught your eye on your mother's bedside table. By high school graduation, you had laid a sturdy enough—or so you thought—cerebral foundation to navigate yourself responsibly and resolutely through the stages of adult development ahead.

Back then, the process of making headway in life was pretty clear-cut. Whenever you had an objective in mind for furthering yourself—from enhancing your diet and people skills to securing a job, life partner, or first piece of real estate—you went through a trusty series of steps to ensure the right outcome:

- See the big picture.
- Decide what you want.

- Consider various routes.
- Narrow down the alternatives.
- Think through consequences.
- Settle on a course of action.
- Implement your strategy.
- Sustain toward the finish line.
- Enjoy your new destination.
- Repeat when a new personal improvement goal appears on the horizon.

And then it all got complicated.

As the internet boom hit in the early nineties and the world started to get a whole lot flatter, you suddenly had access to a selection of everything from music, books, recipes, and medical advice to personal and professional contacts, job prospects, and ways of life beyond what you'd ever imagined. The middle-of-the-road assortment of products, pastimes, and perspectives you'd grown up on swiftly snowballed into a limitless variety of options for stimulating and advancing yourself on every level. And before long, the new message was clear: anything is possible, literally just a click away, if only you have the confidence to go for it and the time to cram it all in.

To meet the challenge of moving forward in an era of seemingly unbounded potential, you did what had served you so capably in the past. But when you attempted to apply those faithful steps to success that had always worked so well to get you from one level to the next, you felt strangely frazzled and unsure. Chalking up your distress to a lack of time and self-assurance, rather than reading it as a call to renovate your inner foundation for achievement, you looked to time management, stress reduction, and confidence-building strategies to get your go-getting groove back.

Now, as the dizzying array of choices grows ever larger and the gadgets for communicating those options ever more insistent, you may suspect that feeling persistently under the gun has less to do with a shortage of time and positive self-talk than you initially thought. The real reason you feel continually rushed and deficient despite all your efforts to shrink stress, crunch your calendar, and blast through fear and doubt is that you've been trying to retrieve your sense of control with superficial tactics that provide only temporary respite. You haven't gotten to the root of the problem. Like many worn-out yet wise adults, you are starting to see that the key to success in these busy times is not to outsmart the madness—clearly a futile effort—but to go within and restructure your mind-set to make the madness your friend.

This book is all about letting go of what's not working anymore, clearing your head of all those supposed solutions you've been inundated with that are only adding to the clamor, and paving the way to what we all seek: genuinely centered composure amid the clatter of constant change. In this book, I will give you a basic road map for revitalizing that adult brain you developed in adolescence so that it can once again perform for you in a way that makes you feel good about who you are and where you're going.

I'll begin by explaining why this do it all, have it all, be it all era is actually an invitation to live more fully in line with your inner inclinations—if you accept it as something to support you rather than something to overcome. Then I'll show you how trusting your innate wisdom over the cacophony of "expert" opinions out there can help you to feel much more empowered. You'll learn what today's achievement-oriented young adults already know—that the world can be more your oyster than ever before if you surrender to forces beyond your control, become sharply discerning, focus on your strongest suits, and deepen your scope. By the time you close this book, you will have established specific expectations, goals, standards, and strategies for your continued growth and development that are simultaneously energizing, workable, and fit for the times. You will have, in other words, brought your brain up to date and recovered your well-earned sense of mastery so that you can stop wrestling with reality and get on with thriving.

{ chapter 1 }
Get Perspective

The lure of nostalgia became clear to me as a young girl when my grandfather showed me a book called *The Good Old Days, They Were Terrible.* A satirical statement on the American tendency to complain about the status quo and look back longingly at supposedly better times, this book illuminated the past with what you might call mud-covered glasses. Was life really simpler without such enlightened luxuries as air conditioning, deodorant, proper sewage systems, washers and dryers, antibiotics, and child labor laws? Not by a long shot. But many of us find it preferable to reflect wistfully on times gone by, recalling the Hallmark images and leaving out all the hardship and heartbreak, than to focus on adapting to the fruits of our hard-won progress.

Americans crave adventure and advancement, but we don't like having to adjust to the new circumstances created when we find concrete ways to enhance our lives. We often oppose the very conditions we've worked so hard to produce because transition requires us to let go of the known and venture into strange and at first unsettling territory. It's easier, in the short-run anyway, to idealize the past than to train ourselves to get with a modernized, and usually better, program. The downside of resisting the inevitable is that it takes about the same amount of energy as adaptation but it doesn't get you anywhere; it just keeps you stuck and spinning.

The very basis of embracing the information era and having it work for you is being receptive to it. Only by viewing your predicament squarely, from the standpoint that this stage of history like every other stage offers good and bad and a lot of gray in between, will you be able to appreciate and apply the essence of this book. You can begin to improve a situation only when you have a balanced, informed perception of what you're confronting.

The straight, unvarnished truth is that American life will always be largely marked by an ever-increasing need to come to grips with quickening change and expanding choices. If you feel like a pioneer, imagine the early 1800s when the first railway system furthered the concept of transport from "my town to your town by horse" to "my state to your state by train." Or consider all those townspeople whose definition of variety catapulted in a flash from "what's in the general store" to "what's in the Sears Roebuck warehouse" when the first mail order catalogs arrived at the turn of the century. Yes, information is multiplying, technology is advancing, and diversity is expanding at a pace never seen before, but let's face it: progress-related acceleration and accompanying stress is as American as Fourth of July fireworks, Ben Franklin, and apple pie.

By welcoming perpetual change and transition as a positive force that has led to air travel, vaccines, and myriad other marvels that have made life easier, you can lighten the load of adjusting to the benefits of "too much information." Try for a moment to focus on just one humanitarian highlight of living in a time where any kind of information can be accessed or sent without leaving the house: Severely shy, disabled, or sick people can participate in conversations and activities they used to feel shut out of. Abused children can learn what's right or wrong at home by doing a quick Google search. Like-minded people can find each other no matter how obscure their tastes or how many miles between them. Now, how do you feel? Probably less overwhelmed and more optimistic, which frees up the energy needed to further evolve your mind-set in a way that will make your life easier.

Acknowledging what's good about being alive at a time when literally no opportunity is off limits doesn't mean denying the quandaries this freedom has brought. There is no getting away from the discouraging truth that many of us feel overpowered by technology, pressured to do it all, have it all, be it all, and chronically short on downtime and breathing space. And there's no disputing that many Americans are overweight, isolated, and polarized as a result of too much computer use and not enough face-to-face interaction and physical activity. But seeing the benefits *along with* the problems is more productive than seeing just the difficulties. It's reality-based optimism that always inspires solutions.

Now that you know the benefits of a perspective that embraces the full spectrum of advantages and liabilities, you can begin the process of slowly but surely advancing your current point of view to one that works more effectively to bring you satisfaction. Seeing your circumstances with fresh, more objective eyes is the best place to start.

Apply the Wisdom

- Pretend that you have gone back in time and you are a child again. You are looking into the future, into your present life, and you are amazed at what you see. From your childhood perspective, what do you find most incredible about this era, most promising about your adult life as it is right now?

- Imagine that it's 30 years from now and you're looking back at this time in American history. What are you reminiscing about? What do you recall most fondly? What are you most nostalgic about? What do you realize in retrospect that you wished you'd understood when you were living it?

- This chapter has mentioned just a few reasons why "too much information" is a good thing. Take a moment to brainstorm additional ways that recent advancements have made American life—and your life in particular—easier.

{ chapter 2 }
Wake Up to What's Not Working

Carl Allen and Rose Lorkowski are going nowhere. Carl is bored with his job at a bank, cynical after his divorce, and unmotivated to put energy into improving his circumstances. Rose is a single mother, in a dead-end job cleaning houses, in a one-way relationship with a married man, with her self-esteem running on empty. Carl is captivated at a motivational seminar where he is told that his life will get better if he simply says yes to every opportunity that comes his way. Rose is counting on positive self-talk to change her luck; every day she looks in the mirror and repeats to herself something like, "I am strong and beautiful and powerful."

Carl and Rose aren't real people. They're characters in two recent movies—Jim Carrey plays Carl in *Yes Man* and Amy Adams plays Rose in *Sunshine Cleaning*. Their stories are worth telling because they demonstrate, albeit in exaggerated ways, why so many achievement-oriented American adults are unhappy. Saying yes to everything certainly gets Carl out of his rut, but he adds to his problems by being too open to opportunity. Rose finds that trying to convince herself of what she wishes were true just amplifies the gap between who she is and who she wants to be.

Carl is a comical example of adults who exacerbate their already complex lives by being overly amenable to personal and professional growth adventures. Options for getting to the next level, no matter how evolved you already are, are promoted everywhere. Inundated with the message that we must continually augment our lives to be okay, we feel downright lazy if we're not actively involved in some sort of effort to move forward. If we're content with where we are or uncertain about where to go next, we figure it must be because we're not facing our deepest fears, unleashing our true capabilities, or being sufficiently open-minded. Distracted from one personal improvement program by the clever marketing of another, we go round and round on the self-help hamster wheel, never asking ourselves if we even want or need the latest reinvention regimen we've robotically bought into.

As Rose demonstrates so well in *Sunshine Cleaning*, another way adults further complicate their lives in their quest for personal improvement is by repeatedly falling for quick fixes. Workshop, book, and magazine titles assure us that it's possible to *ignite your potential, achieve your life purpose, transform your body, deepen your relationships, be the person you were meant to be*—all in *ten easy steps!, within 30 days!, by this weekend!* These promises are irresistible to a culture hooked on instant gratification. If we can send and receive information at once via countless gadgets; download virtually any movie, article, or book; order any product right this minute; or prepare just about any type of food within seconds in the microwave, why can't we experience immediate personal or professional growth, too? Though we're old enough to know better, it's hard to defy the fantasy that we can condense multifaceted life stages, decisions, disappointments, and lessons into fast, pain-free leaps.

Thanks to the two-hour time frame imposed by Hollywood, Jim Carrey's Carl realizes fairly quickly that the trick to being happy is to think through personal growth options and say yes only to what truly appeals to him. And faced with the futility of forcing optimism through rote affirmations, Amy Adams's Rose sees that she will feel better about herself only when she rolls up her sleeves and literally gets down to the tough business of cleaning up her messy life.

But what about the rest of us?

Most responsible adults are overly caught up in personal improvement because we're convinced we're not adequate as we are, we're searching for an elusive panacea, or both. Common to these three situations is the misguided conviction that no human dilemma is too big for convenient, one-size-fits-all approaches. We have come to believe that major life changes are like baking a cake, treating a cold, creating a budget, or tackling a home improvement project. They can be accomplished merely by downloading the instructions, picking up the appropriate *Idiot's Guide*, or consulting the right expert.

Unfortunately, quick fix approaches are largely ineffective interventions for personal or professional development because they don't allow for the true integration that is critical to lasting learning. Reading ten-easy-steps articles or books or listening to a charismatic self-help guru talk can certainly be enlightening and exciting, but information alone, no matter how fired up you are, won't do the trick. Bona fide transformation happens when information is applied consistently, step by habit-building step, over time, and only when the tactics and techniques for change ring true for you.

There are infinite ways to improve your life — repeating affirmations, meditating, doing yoga, eating healthfully, getting rid of clutter, getting organized, focusing on what you appreciate, and so on. But the catch is that none of these perfectly legitimate, widely accessible approaches will make a dent if applied haphazardly, out of guilt or obligation, on top of an already overloaded schedule, or for any reason other than that the approach totally resonates with you. If you don't really need it, want it, or have room in your life to assimilate it, there's no point in doing it.

So how do you decide what personal improvement efforts to engage in?

You may recall Susan from the preface to this book. She's the nonprofit executive whose life is so congested with personal and professional enhancement strategies that she has lost sight of who she is and what her goals and dreams are.

Susan eventually brought about peace of mind by going on a self-help diet. She swore off all self-help books, magazines, blogs, and seminars for six months to clear her head. It was tough at first to withdraw from the steady stream of advice to which she'd become addicted, but she found that the longer she stayed on the diet, the more clearly she saw what she really wanted and needed, not just in terms of self-help but in all aspects of her life.

Jack, a forty-something attorney, came to me for therapy because he had recently gone through a bitter divorce and become irritable, forgetful, and disorganized at work—to the point where his boss had called him on his need to get his life in check. Jack was invested in pulling himself together, but he had no idea how he could work in exercising, eating better, slowing his mind down, processing his anger, and all the other strategies he'd researched that he knew would help him.

The solution for Jack was to start gradually, selecting and experimenting with one new self-improvement approach at a time and sticking with it long enough to see if it suited him. His initial fear was that just one approach wouldn't be enough, but he soon realized that less is sometimes more. His commitment to a weekly divorce support group for two months helped Jack to feel calmer and more positive, and better able to choose the next self-improvement step. By taking on just one self-improvement goal at a time, rather than dividing his attention and energy among several approaches, Jack was able to greatly reduce his stress level and feel much more centered.

Apply the Wisdom

- Make a list of all the self-improvement approaches you've ever tried, are currently involved with, or are thinking about taking on. Put the list away for a couple of days and contemplate which approaches really, truly resonate with you. Then circle your top three and ask yourself which of those three you really, truly have the time, energy, and passion for.

- Consider where you get the most pressure to improve yourself. Are you overly influenced by certain TV shows, magazines, blogs, celebrities, friends and co-workers, relatives, your own high standards? Think hard about the messages you're getting from these sources and ask yourself if you really need to follow through on all or any of them. Consider cutting out the sources of unwanted, unnecessary advice.

- Make a list of important self-improvement aspirations that have eluded you. Perhaps you've always wanted to be more assertive, lose weight, think more positively, or be more organized. Ask yourself honestly if maybe you haven't achieved these goals simply because you've wanted too quick a fix or haven't allowed sufficient space in your schedule to get lasting results. If you feel that a more reasonable approach might make the difference, consider trying again.

{ chapter 3 }
Put Yourself in Charge

Recently I got lost while driving to a speaking engagement. I'd downloaded directions from MapQuest. They seemed pretty simple, but I just couldn't find the building I wanted. I kept going over the directions, thinking that maybe I'd misread them somehow, because it seemed highly unlikely that the universal navigation "expert" could be wrong. Finally, out of sheer frustration, I stopped at a convenience store for advice and learned that MapQuest should have directed me to turn right from the expressway exit instead of left.

Shortly after this incident, I read a news magazine article about the alarming number of mishaps that have resulted from inaccurate GPS instructions. The article described several horrible accidents, including the head-on collision of a car into an oncoming train because the driver blindly obeyed erroneous GPS instructions to turn left onto the train tracks.

What both of these examples illustrate quite literally is that you may not reach your destination—on the pavement or the road of life—if you rely only on external directions to get you there. Having infinite advice and instructions available in a culture that is rich with technology and information can be hugely efficient, but only if we allow ourselves to have the final say. The more we empower outside factors, from the cheerleading of self-help sages to the so-called foolproof electronic voice emanating from the GPS, to pilot us, the less in touch we become with our own innate sense of direction.

In all matters of life and work, discovering where you want to go and how you want to get there starts with making you the ultimate decision maker. And that means appointing your intuition to be your most trustworthy compass. You might assume that you can rely less on your inner sense of direction when you have access to so many sources of guidance, but the truth is that you need your intuition more than ever to sort through all the options before you and pinpoint the routes that are best for you.

Intuition is the act of knowing or sensing without using rational processes. Though intuition is often regarded in our society as a gift unique to women, I have found consistently in my work with both genders that intuition is an experience of inner knowing, an intangible personal adviser, and a faithful barometer common to men *and* women.

Intuition comes forth in many ways. It's that "I just knew" sensation people describe when, after years of bad dates, they have that sudden surreal experience of stumbling upon "the one." It's the slight but sure discomfort you feel when you can't put your finger on what's wrong with a career or real estate opportunity that by all objective standards adds up but for some vague reason doesn't feel quite right. It's what led you to this book, and what is helping you decide what to take with you and make your own from each chapter.

Randy, a very busy accountant, came to me for therapy because he'd recently called off his wedding to a woman he'd realized in the final hour wasn't right for him. He cited proposing to the wrong woman as evidence that he was too wrapped up in his grueling workload to reflect sufficiently on major life choices. His dilemma led to an exploration of how he could step away from his professional demands to make better personal decisions, and I asked him to recall the last time he'd consulted his intuition. He thought carefully, taking long sips from the fancy Starbucks drink he'd brought with him to my office, and concluded regretfully that not only could he not think of a single example, but he didn't think he even had intuition. Pointing to his Starbucks confection, I asked, "So tell me: why did you buy that coffee drink?" "I don't know," he replied, "I didn't think about it. I just knew it would make me feel better so I bought it." And that, I said, is your intuition at work.

Your intuition—from telling you what menu item to choose to whether someone is telling you the truth—is with you, ready with unflagging leadership and never faltering through situations mundane to magical. Its unassuming voice, however, often gets crowded out by the squeakier sources of advice—ingrained childhood beliefs, the media, family members, co-workers—clamoring for attention.

Fortunately, intuition is unrelenting and unshakable in its desire to lead you toward fulfilling your innermost wishes and goals. It communicates with you inventively through dreams, images, gut reactions, and signs. Ever undeterred and resourceful, your intuition lets you know through synchronicities, coincidences, and an ever-growing sense of encouragement when you're on the right track, and via escalating accidents, physical symptoms, and a general aura of anxiety and dread when you're not.

Here's an example of how intuition gets through to you when you ignore it.

Mark had a sense when he accepted a competitive position at an advertising agency known as a "sweat shop" that, despite the great salary, this wasn't the right fit for him. His initial discomfort proved telling when, after a few months in his new job, he found himself feeling irritable, exhausted, and jumpy from too much work and too little sleep. His intuition attempted to let him know—through his worsening mood and daily mishaps—that his current direction was not furthering his satisfaction with life. But he kept right on going, convincing himself that he'd be a fool to throw away such a coveted career opportunity.

Then one day, fighting traffic to get to work on time, chugging a Red Bull to wake himself up, he pressed the wrong pedal and slammed his brand new car into a truck at a stop sign. That's when his faith in his intuition finally kicked in. Jarred by a red flag as blatant as a traffic calamity, he finally realized that the growing voice inside him meant business. It was his unfamiliarity with his intuition that had made him miss the building mayhem in all areas of his life as a glaring intuitive sign that he was going down the wrong path.

The great thing about intuition is that it's ready to start working for you just as soon as you're ready to count on it. No matter how long it takes you to come to your senses and heed its astute insights, your intuition is always certain and steady. Intuition doesn't get weird when you don't listen; but it doesn't let up either, even when you try with all your might to drown it out. Eventually impressed by its steadfast loyalty, you believe in it enough to act on it. With each step you take, you feel rewarded. You experience an increasing sense of well-being, and so trust grows. The more you pay attention to your intuition, the more powerful and creative it becomes in smoothing the way to what makes you feel the truest sense of being alive.

Dana has what we'd call a mature relationship with her intuition. She learned as a young girl that she could rely on her intuition to send her navigational messages through physical sensations. When she had a stomachache, she knew that something in her life was amiss and needed her assistance. When she felt like smiling, she knew she was in a situation where it was okay to be herself and relax. By her early twenties, Dana's trust in her intuition was so committed that she just knew that no matter what her dilemma, her intuition would always come through with just the right answer at just the right time.

In her early thirties, Dana was perfectly satisfied with the life she had built for herself in her home state of Kansas but for some inexplicable reason longed to live in the Northeast. Though she'd never been to that part of the country, she had a particular hunch about Maine. While mulling over her instinct at a stoplight in Topeka one day, she found herself staring at a Maine license plate on the car ahead.

Recognizing this as an undeniable sign from her intuition to relocate, she moved east and started a life that felt even more right than the successful one she'd left. She'd thought she had "it all" in Topeka with a great job and wonderful friends. Had she not trusted the whisper of her intuition, she would not have ended up meeting her husband and discovering she loved mountains and the sea even more than the Midwest plains.

Intuition is a great guide and teacher because it always pulls us toward situations that nourish our sense of comfort with ourselves and the world. But, like most of what propels us toward personal growth, the challenge sometimes of getting to a broader place can be disruptive and frightening. The tough thing about intuition isn't so much figuring out what it has to say; it's summoning the courage to act on it. And that, of course, is why we do so much to distract ourselves from really hearing what sorts of risks we might have to take if we really want to rise to the potential our intuition is always turning us toward.

A really hard part about developing a relationship with our intuition is that our quick-fix, stimulation-addicted culture makes little space for small voices and subtle signs. Because intuition refuses to compete with speed or flash, you have to pause from the attention-impaired frenzy of American life and consciously create situations that encourage your intuition to speak with you. If you don't pause, you won't be able to respect intuitive messages that may not seem logical because you'll be too inundated with outside distractions to believe in something that makes sense only to you. Building a relationship with your intuition demands that you simultaneously start letting go of what others think and trusting that, even when the messages seem half-baked and you may look crazy to others for following them, your intuition is always leading you in the direction of improved circumstances. And you are never obligated to explain it.

Following your intuition takes sheer guts and faith at times. Being true to your inner voice means being able to take such courageous actions as uprooting yourself from a perfectly comfortable (but not quite stimulating) relationship or job with nothing else lined up. It means believing in yourself so completely that nothing can get in the way of what you know, that when your intuition tells you to do something, even if it seems insane and the step will create emotional upheaval, you will ultimately be better off.

Intuition, because it is sparked from within by sheer self-confidence, always thrives in an atmosphere of self-care. So it's really quite matter of fact: if you want your intuition to flourish, treat yourself well. That means doing what you want to do because you want to do it, not because you feel swayed to do it by some outside force. It means being open to the right opportunities for learning and growth. It means balancing your life with ample doses of solitude so that your intuition can rise up and be heard. Mostly, it means refusing to let fear stop you from making changes that you know will make you the person you want to be.

As you move further along in this book, you will find yourself using your intuition more and more to whittle your life down to what's most important, find calm in the storm, dismiss circumstances that don't truly suit you, and attract situations that are more in line with who you are at your core. You may already be getting strong internal messages about the direction you want to go in—or maybe you're just beginning to break the ice with your intuition. Either way, you are right where you need to be at this moment.

Upcoming chapters will give you plenty of opportunity to become better acquainted with your intuition. For now, remember: intuition responds more to gentle coaxing than pressure to perform. It's just a matter of slowing down and giving your intuition a warm, inviting welcome. And what I mean by slowing down is making your focus right now on noticing what your intuition has to say.

This is not the time to worry about acting on your intuition. When you worry about the unsettling transitions you might have to go through if you take your intuition seriously, such as breaking up with someone or starting a new career in order to be happier at the other end, fear of change is likely to shut your intuition right down. What you most need to know now is that a gradual, step-by-step courtship is the way to go. Have fun getting to know your intuition better. I promise that I'll help you get more clear on what you want and deal with your fears about taking action soon enough.

Apply the Wisdom

- Look back on your life and consider what smart decisions have come from following your instincts and what poor decisions have come from not acting when something seemed off. Consider how your life would be different if you'd followed your gut at those times when you disregarded it. Also consider how your life might look in, let's say, three years if you listen to your intuition from now on.

- Spend a day resolving to take direction from your intuition whenever possible. Stop and ask before you go through the usual motions: Am I eating cereal for breakfast this morning because I really want cereal or because eating cereal is a habit? Am I agreeing to have lunch with this person out of obligation or because I truly enjoy their company? At the end of the day, notice how you feel and what you learned.

- Ask your intuition for a few suggestions on what you can do to make your life less overwhelming. What might you let go of? What might you bring in?

- Ask your intuition how you can create more time and space in your life to let it communicate with you. See what messages you receive.

{ chapter 4 }
Take Care of the Basics First

I vividly remember being in the middle of my doctorate program, working hard and fast to reach graduation. At the patient urging of my intuition over many years, I had returned to school at age 30 in the midst of a lucrative but unfulfilling publishing career. Though I was absolutely sure psychology was my calling despite the financial sacrifice, daunting workload, and uncertain future, the way I was approaching it felt all wrong to me. Putting myself through the rigorous program I'd enrolled in was taking its toll to the point where I'd abandoned many of the practices that had helped me to be successful in the past. I had become so exhausted and single-focused in my effort to turn myself into a psychologist that I'd lost touch with what is primary to every kind of success: personal well-being.

I came to my senses one day at school when, as usual, the conversation around me centered on panic and competition. My classmates and I would chatter frantically about what our professors were always drilling into us: there'd be a shortage of psychologist positions upon graduation and only the cream of the crop would get hired. Like my peers, I'd been doing everything possible to stay above the curve and stand out. I'd filled my course schedule to the hilt to demonstrate my stamina, taken on extra demanding training stints and completed them early to show my grit, gotten straight As at all costs to confirm my command of the material. I felt added pressure to prove myself because, unlike many of my classmates who'd worked in psychology prior to pursuing their doctorates, I was starting at square one.

My head was such a swirl of new learning, anxiety about my future, and pressure to keep up that I had to take medication to sleep at night, and I looked and felt tense all the time. Because I was going to class, studying, or training every hour of the day, every day of the week, there was no time to socialize, exercise, or unwind. I kept myself going by eating and drinking in quick bursts—an energy bar here, a cup of coffee there, fast food on the run.

As I stood in the student lounge that day, wired from another night of tossing and turning, unconsciously readying myself for the usual cutthroat academic atmosphere, the typical frantic kibitzing among my classmates suddenly turned into a distant droning buzz. A distinct picture appeared in my mind. I felt unexpectedly grounded. I imagined my future employer, a gifted veteran psychologist, choosing from two recent graduates to hire: one candidate completely frazzled and fried from trying too hard to stand out, the other candidate appearing calm and composed from having moved through the hurdles of graduate school at a sensible pace.

I knew in that instant which candidate I wanted to be.

On that pivotal day in graduate school, I realized that even the most stellar report card, letter of reference, or resumé wouldn't help me succeed if I were too worn down by fear and competition to effectively apply the knowledge represented on paper. Worrying about an unpredictable job market was not going to help me, nor would obsessively comparing myself to my peers, pushing myself to produce at an unreasonable rate, or participating in negative, draining conversation. There would always be competition, and there would always be some new accolade to shoot for. Getting too wrapped up in all that would only make me less viable. Graduate school was hard enough, and I was making it all the harder with my fear-based, overly self-conscious approach to getting through it.

My epiphany that day was that my best strategy for landing a good job after graduation would be to act in line with becoming that calm, composed, and confident job candidate I'd just seen in my mind. Right then and there I vowed to disengage from the pessimistic chatter at school and put my time and energy to better use. Instead of striving to outdo my classmates, I tried from that point forward to eat balanced meals again, take a night off every week to laugh with my friends, refresh myself with brisk walks between study sessions, and wind down a little earlier at night to encourage sleep. Graduate school remained very difficult, and I still had serious moments of doubt and inadequacy, but as I increasingly made the fundamentals of healthy functioning my top priority, I felt better equipped to deal with the challenges at hand. And, as I'd hoped, I did end up feeling calm and confident after graduation. Despite the stiff competition and my inexperience compared to my peers, I got hired for the job I most wanted—not because my resumé rose to the top, but because, in the words of my interviewer, my personality seemed "down to earth."

Granted, graduate school is not an everyday experience causing stress for American adults, but the most common theme among my clients by far is the need to learn what I've just described: if you take care of yourself first, you will be in a much better to position to accomplish what is important to you.

In a world fixated on external productivity and one-upsmanship, it is easy to get caught up in the notion that taking time away from work for the sake of maintaining your sense of well-being will slow your progress, make you less in demand, and leave you left out. But the truth is that if you don't get enough sleep, nutrients, fresh air, exercise, or positive social interaction, you will eventually run out of steam. You have only so much time and energy, and that time and energy will go further if you channel some of it into making sure your basic needs are taken care of before you address anything else.

Apply the Wisdom

- Keeping your head in the sand is a bad idea. You need to know unpleasant truths—a road is closed, a storm is coming, the economy is melting down, the job market is limited, your career skill set is outdated, etc.—in order to prepare for the future. But obsessing over unsettling news is counterproductive. Are you going over the negatives unnecessarily? If so, identify the sources—the nightly news, pessimistic friends or colleagues, an overly cynical blog—and consider cutting down or shutting off access. Then see if your outlook improves.

- Ask yourself honestly: are you doing your best to take care of yourself? What small changes can you make to sleep more soundly, eat more healthfully, feel more comfortable in your body? Contemplate whatever it is you need to do to be better rested and more centered.

- Is there an area of your life where you're feeling inexplicitly out of sorts? Are you less secure or passionate at work or in an important relationship than you used to be and not sure why? Perhaps it's the pace that's the problem. Ask yourself if you've gotten out of a once resonant rhythm because you feel external pressure to go faster or pile more on. Would you feel more yourself and thus more effective if you took a stand and started to get back to your old rhythm?

{ chapter 5 }
Approach Your Development as a Work in Progress

Early on in private practice, I started to notice a definite trend. Adults in their thirties and forties would come to me protesting that they were falling short of what their parents had accomplished by their age. The common complaint would go something like this: "When my dad was 30, he'd been working at the same company for 12 years, my mom didn't work, and they had two kids, a mortgage, and a retirement plan, and two cars in the garage. I just broke up with my girlfriend. I can't seem to stick with one job, and I'm still renting an apartment with no money in the bank. What's wrong with me?" Or this: "My mom was happily married with three kids, a beautiful home and a summer cottage, and strong community ties when she was my age, and I'm just starting to figure things out. I've been a bridesmaid ten times, and I can't find a decent guy or a job I'm passionate about. I've always wanted to get married and have kids; and it's just not happening."

As a freshly minted psychologist when I started to hear these stories, I could certainly relate. At 35, I was single with a new career in a new city, renting an apartment, just getting back on my financial feet after paying for my education. Like the adults coming to me for advice, I was nowhere near where my parents had been at my age, and I couldn't even imagine how I would ever own a home, meet Mr. Right, or be fiscally solvent. Where my parents had been settled in and squared away in their thirties, I was a new kid on the block just starting out.

What struck me as I considered my own situation and listened to numerous adults describe feeling unfulfilled and lacking because they couldn't reach certain milestones of adult development as easily as their parents had was that all of us were gauging our progress with an outdated blueprint. There was a time when adult development happened in linear fashion, moving through concrete stages fairly predictably. In general, American adults went from high school or college graduation to marriage to buying a house to having and raising children to retirement—with one spouse, one or two jobs in the same career, in one or two houses; with one loyal group of family, friends, and neighbors.

If you worked hard and kept your commitments, following this conventional course from early adulthood to death would yield increasingly fulfilling parts of the American Dream. Lucrative promotions in exchange for long-term company loyalty. Satisfying returns on retirement and college investments. Home equity. Financial flexibility and spending power. Deepening community involvement. The longer you stayed on course, the more rewards you reaped. And if you didn't stay the course, maybe because your marriage or career wasn't working out despite your best intentions or because you decided you preferred a warm climate to a cold one, that meant you were a job-hopper, wishy-washy, a home wrecker, or worse.

From approximately the World War II years until the beginning of the Reagan era, the path of adult development was mostly predictable because corporate America was more reliable, supportive institutions like churches and family were more solid, the American dollar was robust, and options for adult development were less visible. It was simpler for young adults to launch themselves confidently and resolutely into the world when there were fewer discernible lifestyle and career options to choose from and the framework for conventional success—resilient banks, nuclear families, big companies, respected places of worship—was sturdy and strong.

The rules of living the American Dream have changed dramatically over the last 20 years or so as corporate, financial, and religious America have become much less dependable and as lifestyle and career choices have snowballed. Adults comparing themselves to past generations when assessing their success must take into account that our parents may have selected a specific life route and stayed with it because they didn't know other routes existed *and* they usually didn't have to worry about outside factors like corporate downsizing and plummeting stocks upending their well-laid plans. The secret to success then was making a commitment and sticking with it. The secret to success now is being ever prepared to adjust to constantly changing circumstances and increasing choices.

The good news is that if you can move beyond the expectation that adult development is an inevitable, straightforward process, you can free yourself from having to achieve certain standards on a certain timeline to feel accepted. Thankfully, the emphasis now is for adults to be who they want to be deep down—whether that's employee or entrepreneur, married or single; with children or without; gay or straight; a country mouse or city mouse—to feel worthy and whole. Yes, not being able to count on the economy or narrow and distinct social norms for a sense of security or affirmation can certainly trigger anxiety. But customizing your life blueprint from within, evaluating your progress according to your own adjustable terms, is what builds the kind of composure that can weather the ever-changing conditions around you.

As varied adult development becomes more the norm, I'm starting to see a new and encouraging trend with, interestingly, my young adult clients. Women and men in their twenties are expressing a liberated approach to adult development in modern times. Natalie, a recent college graduate, says, "I majored in architecture but I'm not sure I'll stick to that. I'm going to try and stay at my job for a year and then maybe I'll join the Peace Corps, and then go into teaching." Josh, out of college five years now with an English degree, says, "I'm thinking about moving back home for a while to save money for graduate school. I've tried a few different jobs and I think I want to do something to help the environment but I'm not sure what. I love my girlfriend but we're not ready for marriage yet."

Natalie and Josh both feel confident about their life decisions, and meandering and taking their time seems like a clever way to explore wide-ranging options, rather than a sign of confusion or an inability to keep up with their peers. So what brought them both to therapy? Not surprisingly, they're having trouble convincing their 40-something parents that their ambling developmental style is normal and healthy.

What established adults can learn from smart young adults like Natalie and Josh is that fulfillment in adulthood comes from looking at your life as a unique work in progress instead of as a well-worn pathway toward a definite finish line. In light of ever-changing outside influences on your inner inclinations, even your most secure decisions may not make sense when newer and better options appear on the horizon. A once sound career choice may not seem as sensible in the face of new technology that could make your job obsolete in five years. Vows you made at the altar may not hold as true when you find yourself, supported by an ever more unprejudiced society, feeling attracted to someone of the same sex. Plans to raise your family in your hometown may give way when once rooted family members and friends move away to pursue greener pastures. There's no telling what events might lead you to change your life course, but one thing is certain: if you don't transform yourself in response to external forces and internal longings, you will not feel fulfilled.

Successful adulthood today requires looking at your life as painter's canvas. That means starting with a general idea of where you're going and trusting that the picture will emerge little by little, day by day, year by year. You paint when inspired, and every now and then you step away and view the big picture. Sometimes you notice that something is missing or that a color you thought was just right is now all wrong. You regularly take breaks from painting to get perspective, and you come back with fresh ideas, ready to make new adjustments that will take your piece of art to the next level, knowing full well that what you apply with confidence one day may not fit at all the next.

Coming up with a vision. Being in the flow of creating. Revisiting what you've committed to. Correcting your mistakes. Standing back and assessing again. Letting multiple sources inspire you. Refining your vision. Altering your strategy. It's all part of the process. Successful adult development starts with letting go of the worn-out idea that adulthood is a written-in-stone itinerary. Finding fulfillment is about being the artist of your own, always-evolving life. Revisiting your goals and dreams regularly to ensure that they still fit who you are and what you want will keep you moving toward an outcome that is right for you.

Apply the Wisdom

- What is your theory of adult development and where did it come from? Consider all the sources that have shaped and continue to shape the standards you aspire to as you grow. Are you adhering to worn-out benchmarks? If so, might you be better off with new and more appropriate criteria for assessing your progress?

- Are there particular areas of your life that you're not happy with? Ask yourself if you could be more content in these areas if you let associated expectations come from within rather than from other people.

- Consider what you have accomplished in your life beyond the expectations that your parents had for you. Maybe you don't have all the trappings of the American Dream but you have greater self-awareness than your parents did, you are more well traveled, you are a bigger risk taker, or you have a more diverse group of friends than they had at your age. Take into account the benefits of being an adult during an era when personal reinvention rules over convention.

- How might your life have played out differently if you'd been born 30 years earlier? What opportunities might you have missed out on if you'd entered adulthood when the hallmarks of maturity were more uniform?

- Close your eyes and visualize yourself as an artist of your own life. Step away from your life canvas, take a long, lingering look, and get a bird's-eye view. Imagine how you want your life to look. What small touch up, revision, or alteration could you make to bring your life just a tiny bit closer to the ultimate work of art you envision?

{ chapter 6 }
Shape Your Development

Every so often when I'd visit my grandparents as a young child, my grandfather would hand me a shiny quarter and say, "Let's go to the penny candy store." I recall the delicious anticipation I'd feel as we'd stroll hand in hand the two blocks to the store. We'd push open the door and a bell would jingle, and we'd walk into a colorful, intoxicating sea of every kind of candy imaginable, all displayed in wicker baskets on long tables that I was just tall enough to reach.

The proprietor would greet us warmly, I'd give her my quarter, and she'd hand me a small paper bag to fill up. Then she and my grandfather would chat leisurely while I took my good sweet time walking slowly around the tables, carefully considering the contents of each basket, and selecting the 25 pieces of candy that appealed to me most. On our walk home, I'd feel entirely confident that the little paper bag I carried was stuffed with the very finest our penny candy store had to offer—because having spent my quarter as judiciously as possible, I knew that every single piece was unquestionably the best candy for me.

My penny candy store memories got me especially excited when my parents bought a bookstore during my sophomore year of high school. A prolific reader, I imagined that having a bookstore in the family would be heaven on earth because I'd have access to any book at any time at no cost. But to my dismay, having an endless selection of books to choose from ended up causing me a great deal of stress. Because I knew I could read absolutely anything, I could never focus on whatever book I'd chosen. Taunted by the thousands of other books that I'd left on the shelves, I was constantly wondering if I'd selected the right book, if maybe I shouldn't be reading what I'd selected because another book might be even better. Hot off the press shipments of potentially enthralling books were always arriving, so I never felt absolutely sure that the book of the moment was the best pick for me.

Not surprisingly, I actually felt relieved when my parents got out of the book business after my college graduation. Finally, the pressure to read only the undeniably most suitable *of it all* was gone. I felt oddly protected when once again there were certain limits in place—what was available at the library, how much money I had in my budget—to sort out my reading choices.

Too many rules can be stifling, but insufficient guidance can create profound pressure. What I've learned from my childhood adventures with candy, my adolescent dilemma with books, and a lot of other decision-making lessons since those times is that the best choices are made when appropriate guidelines are in place. Why did I fare much better choosing candy with a 25-piece quota than I did trying to narrow down books from an infinite inventory? Because good decisions are made with a healthy balance of structure and freedom.

One major challenge of adulthood—especially in a culture that inundates us with the message that we can have whatever we want and be whoever we wish if only we have the stamina to go out and make it all happen—is to restrict the seemingly unbounded array of options for growth into a stimulating yet manageable agenda. While it is exhilarating to think of adult development as filling in a blank canvas, such a no holds barred image can bring on the expectation that we should fill the canvas seamlessly, flawlessly, perfectly—which of course is not humanly possible and can cause incredible anxiety.

When contemplating what actions to take, what choices to make, what goals to strive for as you become more of who you want to be, the following preliminary guidelines will help you to take the opportunities that feel best, leave the rest, and still feel like you're making the most of your life.

Accept that you will never get it all done. You've probably noticed that the more you get into something, a particular subject in school, for example, or a new hobby, interest or cause, the more there is to know. There is always another level to strive for, a new question that needs answering, a greater understanding to shoot for, a more refined approach to take, one more piece to add to the collection. As long as you are alive, there will be something left to learn, think about, struggle with, discover, organize, wrap up, get down. Every motivated adult leaves a to-do list behind, but you know what? Somehow the world keeps spinning. Keeping this in mind will help you to admit that, even though our culture tells us otherwise, you really can't do it all or be it all, and that's absolutely okay.

Be clear on the price you're willing to pay. The way it seems from the glib delivery of advertising—*Anyone can have it all. What are you waiting for? Just go for it.*—all you need to accomplish your goals and dreams is a can-do attitude. Consequently, it's easy to convince yourself that if you don't have a ripped body; haven't become a musician, chef, or whatever your professional bliss is; or don't have the most envied house in your neighborhood, it's because you lack the brains or guts or ingenuity to get it right. Before you blame yourself for not having it all when having it all seems so within your grasp, consider that you're not getting the full picture. Maybe people who seem to have it all—for example, celebrities flaunting their seemingly effortless enviable lives in media interviews—are wealthy enough to employ coaches, cooks, nannies, personal shoppers, and designers to keep them looking carefree and fabulous. Yes, it's true that you can have pretty much whatever you want these days. But at what monetary cost? Having a firm idea of what you can reasonably afford to spend will help you to make personal growth decisions that fit your lifestyle.

Let your overarching goals lead you. Another important message the media leaves out when prompting us to keep improving ourselves is that certain life "enhancements" may not be in line with what's ultimately most important to you. Maybe it's true that you can have whatever career you fancy, but what if your family is your number-one priority and pursuing your professional passion means less time with your spouse and kids? Perhaps it's perfectly possible for you to make lots more money, but what if you're a highly ethical person and getting a raise means doing work that you don't entirely believe in? Before you jump on an opportunity to supposedly improve your life, check it out carefully to make sure you won't have to compromise that which you hold most vital and dear.

Exercise your right to say enough is enough. In our "new and improved" culture, there is always another option on the horizon for finding fulfillment. Perhaps you've tried every possible route to overcoming infertility, meeting your life partner, finding an acting job, getting over your fear of flying to no avail, and you are exhausted and spent and beyond frustrated. Then suddenly you hear of unexpected hope—the latest fertility treatment, a new internet matchmaking service, a revolutionary phobia cure, yet another audition. You don't feel excited about taking your chances on trying again only to end up disappointed one more time, but you don't want to be branded a failure or be left wondering what if. When there is almost no end in sight to the lengths you can go to solve a problem, it's important to determine from within whether you want to keep at something. There will always be arguments to keep going, to not give up, to stay in the fight, and only you can decide when to draw the line.

Respect where you are in your personal evolution. Just because there are endless opportunities for excitement and adventure doesn't mean they are right for where you are at your age and stage. Perhaps people have told you that you have a real knack for writing, political advocacy, or teaching. You agree, but you don't feel mature enough yet to embark on that path. Or maybe you've always wanted to live in a bustling big city, but you aren't excited about moving to New York to live with your girlfriend because you've become fonder of open spaces and a slower pace as you've grown older. We all change our preferences as we move through life and grow from experience. So look within periodically to make sure that your goals are aligned with where you are developmentally.

Go with what inspires you most. In the end, after you've thought all your options through and been very practical about what life ventures make the most sense, it's really what's calling you from deep down that's most important—even if others don't quite get your reasoning. Let's say you've just been told you're getting downsized at work in a couple of months and common sense insists that you should be looking for a new job, but your intuition is strongly telling you to spend your severance package on an African safari. Or it could be that your house hasn't been updated in 30 years and really could use at least a fresh coat of paint and some new living room furniture, but you really don't care about home improvement. You'd rather spend your time and energy on taking and developing your own photographs. When you follow instructions from within to perk up your life, regardless of whether those instructions seem logical, you will more likely end up in a better place.

Apply the Wisdom

- Consider the most effective guiding principles you have used to accomplish your goals up until now. Do you respond well to lots of structure, or do you prefer lots of leeway? Determining what your comfort zone is between a blank canvas and hard and fast rules will help you to arrive at a style of growth that really works for you.

- Take a look at your personal budget, and consider reworking it to include categories related to improving your life, such as "professional development," "landscaping," "health and fitness," "travel," "entertainment," and any other category that's pertinent to you. Then determine how much money per year you can reasonably spend on each category. See how it feels to use your new budget to narrow down your life choices.

- Think about what you watch, read, and listen to that may be leading you to have life improvement aspirations that don't quite fit your lifestyle. If you want to strive for a lifestyle that will make these goals feasible, find a way to do that. If not, resolve to ignore the out-of-reach self-improvement messages that make you feel you're not trying hard enough.

- Make a list of five adjectives you hope people will use to describe you at the end of your life. Do you want to be remembered as adventurous, loyal, honest, funny, efficient, easy-going, artistic? What words come to mind? The next time you're at a fork in the road, ask yourself which road will take you closer to the adjectives that represent what's most important to you in the long run.

- If you have many life enhancement goals in mind and you're not ready to shorten your list, take a shot at imposing organizational structure that will allow you to work everything in. You could give each month of the year a theme, such as dance, web design, outdoor fun, or gardening, and learn and do everything possible related to the theme of the month. That's just one thought. Experiment a little and see what you come up with.

{ chapter 7 }
Reel Yourself In

At first glance Laura seems to be a pretty fortunate woman. She's worked for the same company for 15 years, steadily moving up, earning new responsibilities and greater rewards at each level. Married 25 years, she is still attracted to her husband. She lives an hour away from her childhood neighborhood where many of her relatives still live. She and her husband actually *look forward to* big cozy birthday and holiday gatherings with extended family.

What makes Laura not so fortunate, despite the cheery images her increasingly rare traditional life description evokes, is that she is plagued with the notion that she is not putting herself out there, pushing herself hard enough, reaching her true potential, creating the life she really deserves. As she explained at our first therapy session, she was content with her life until she could no longer ignore the relentless headlines at the supermarket checkout counter: *Step Outside Your Comfort Zone! Break Out of Your Rut! Isn't It Time to Reinvent Yourself?* As we wound up our first session, she wondered, "Am I happy? Or am I just telling myself I'm happy with my career, my husband, where I live, with my family because I'm in denial about my need for change and am too afraid to take risks?"

Her old-school approach to adult development—staying on one linear track—makes Laura an anomaly, but her situation illustrates a conundrum that most adults can relate to. Even if your life doesn't seem nicely sewn up like Laura's, it's easy to feel like you're avoiding something, hiding out, or lying to yourself if you're not going through some sort of transition. In a culture that encourages inner growth and development from every angle at every turn, how do you distinguish between wanting change because you genuinely need it and wanting change because it's all the rage? And if you determine that change really is necessary, how much change is required to provide improved satisfaction, well-being, confidence, or whatever other lift you're hoping for?

If you were a fan of that classic 1970s Mary Tyler Moore, Bob Newhart, Carol Burnett Saturday night lineup like me, you may remember that *Mary Tyler Moore* episode where Mary feels the need for something new in her life but she can't put her finger on what will break the monotony. Worried that she may have to completely overhaul herself, she is relieved to learn that just moving to a new apartment is enough to make her whole life feel fresh again. Were that episode to air today, my guess is that moving from a vintage apartment house to a high rise wouldn't be enough for Mary—or her viewers. In this day and age, the cure for Mary's doldrums would be something much more dramatic, like getting married in Vegas, coming out of the closet, or perhaps running off with the circus.

Sometimes big change is definitely in order to make a difference. It's great that our culture promotes the idea that it's never too late to leave a dead-end job, get out of a stale marriage, adopt a baby, or do just about anything else to rev up your life. But reinvention is overprescribed by media appealing to America's love of personal transformation stories. So many adults go overboard in their attempts to reach new heights.

If your goal is to be a better cook, you don't have to quit your day job and enroll in a first-class culinary school. If you're bored with your daily routine, you don't have to uproot yourself from everything familiar, move to Tuscany, and start harvesting olives. If you want to reclaim your sense of youthful spontaneity, you don't have to sell your suburban home and travel around the world on a yacht.

Before you choose an extreme life-enhancement measure to turn things around, consider that there may be a simpler choice.

Ross came to me for coaching because he felt the need to leave his sales job and open an antique shop. He'd never been crazy about sales but always figured he'd stick with it because the money was good. Now, after reading an article on a business trip about the importance of finding your true calling, he was convinced that he should take his longstanding passion for antique furniture much more seriously. What Ross ended up realizing through therapy was that working part-time at an antique store was enough to provide the fulfillment he wanted. Being practical five days a week and doing what he loves on Saturday afternoons has turned out to be the perfect combination.

Meredith sought therapy out of concern that her marriage had dried up. She and her husband had two sons, shared values, common goals, and mutual respect, and she had felt satisfied until she tuned into a talk show discussing the trend for women of a certain age to leave their "good enough" husbands to open themselves up to more exciting adventures. When she arrived at my office, she was convinced that she'd have to leave her husband to make her life better. Fortunately, Meredith discovered that she could bring more stimulation into her life by relying on her husband less to fill all of her needs. Enrolling in a wine appreciation class and resolving to socialize with her girlfriends on a weekly basis made her life feel more interesting, and suddenly her marriage had a spark again.

Sometimes, of course, no change is needed, and it's just a matter of getting back in touch with the fact that things are fine just the way they are.

What Laura from the start of the chapter came to terms with in therapy is that she needed more confidence in her capacity to know what is right for her. During the course of our treatment, she was panicked by an unexpected job offer with a higher salary in a bigger city. She felt pressure to accept the job because her friends were forever telling her that she'd been at her current job too long and needed to keep an edge in her field by getting experience in a more competitive market. Persuasive wooing from her potential new employer, along with enthusiasm from her husband and kids, made it hard to resist, but she ultimately decided to trust what she knew deep down. Sure, city life is exciting and this new job could take her career to new places but, trendy or not, she prefers small city life and likes her familiar work environment just fine.

As I grow older and wiser and become more and more discerning about choosing personal and professional growth opportunities for myself, I periodically look back on my college days when I was ready to jump on any and every chance to explore the world and boost my career. At that age I couldn't imagine why anyone would ever decline the chance to get ahead in life or at work, so I was shocked when my musically gifted friend Elizabeth turned down a coveted fellowship with a renowned orchestra to get married and have kids. I thought she was nuts and told her so. Why would anyone say no to a once-in-a-lifetime offer to do something so boring and ordinary? All I could conclude back then was that Elizabeth was too weak and dull to go after what she really wanted and I was the strong, interesting risk taker.

Almost 25 years later, Elizabeth is still happily married to her college boyfriend and has three thriving kids. She is very fulfilled, with no regrets about giving up music to raise a family, *and* she is interesting. Elizabeth and I see eye to eye now because I get where she was coming from when she chose marriage over music at 21. Contrary to what I'd thought at the time, she'd been way ahead of me in college in terms of her ability to hear and act on her intuition despite the criticism of others. What I've learned from this dear friend of mine is that opportunities for growth and change aren't really opportunities if they're not right for you. And quite often standing firm in the face of an opportunity to supposedly move forward is an indication of strength rather than a sign of weakness.

Apply the Wisdom

- Consider what changes, if any, you might want to make with your job, where you live, the company you keep, the way you look, and any other important life area that comes to mind. Ask yourself honestly: of the desired changes you come up with, which of these are suggestions from your gut and which are reactions to outside duress to join the change bandwagon?

- Select one change your inner voice is urging you to make. Are you resisting the change because it seems too big? Scale that change back a bit, and see if a smaller revision will get you the result you want. For example, if you're sure that you've outgrown your job, consider whether taking on a new responsibility at work or involving yourself in a new interest after work might jazz things up sufficiently.

- Look back on opportunities that you've passed up in your life and at work. Maybe you decided not to take a childhood interest like gymnastics or basketball to the next level, or perhaps you turned down a job offer or elected not to join a certain cause or committee. Consider the unexpected benefits that have come from turning these opportunities down. For example, deciding not to become a professional athlete or actor may have brought more balance to your life; choosing not to relocate with your company might have led you down a new career path; saying no to a marriage proposal that didn't feel entirely right may have helped you to respect yourself more.

- Contemplate your definition of "advancement." Consider instances where you have advanced in life and at work from not accepting a supposed "opportunity." For example, maybe you advanced as a parent and partner when you put your career on hold to stay home and run a household. Or you might have advanced in your ability to be committed and focused by saying yes to just one volunteer obligation and saying no to the rest.

{ chapter 8 }
Summon Your Strengths

Erica, a consulting client of mine, is a crackerjack nonprofit fundraiser, so I suggested that she start giving talks on her golden touch at professional conferences. Her response? "I don't really know what I'd have to offer. This stuff is pretty basic." Recently I asked my brother David, a self-taught carpenter who transforms dilapidated old houses into real estate miracles, just how he does it. His reply? "It's common sense." Erica and David share the assumption that if what they're doing comes naturally, without a whole lot of strain, it must not be very noteworthy.

Ingrained in our culture is the idea that satisfaction comes from "grinning and bearing it," "pulling yourself up by the bootstraps," working yourself to the limit to break barriers and accomplish the impossible. American literature is rife with stories about ordinary people who make names for themselves by bravely conquering their doubts and fears and doing against incredible odds what others said they could never do. What we have learned from our heritage of success at all costs is that achievement is respectable only when it demands that we humble and contort ourselves to accomplish it. Gain, as the saying goes, doesn't come without pain.

But actually, the opposite is true.

While worthy accomplishment often does come from tough, punishing labor, you are most likely to succeed when you're doing something that just seems to flow and feel right for you. Think of Michelangelo painting the Sistine Chapel, the Bronte' sisters turning out brilliant novels, and other historical figures who created unforgettable works of art out of pure inspiration. These compelling examples illustrate that the most remarkable feats happen not when you're going against the grain to prove yourself but when you're doing what simply feels comfortable.

It used to be that if you weren't adept at something, you'd get extra instruction in that area. The boss would send the scattered employee to a time management seminar and the shy employee to assertiveness training. In your free time you'd take a dance class to improve your coordination or an auto mechanics course to learn how to fix your own car. The goal was to become well rounded so that you could fill in where needed at work and cover all the bases at home.

Only recently have the experts come to realize that it makes sense to stop wasting energy trying to do what you're not so good at and invest more wisely in becoming even better at what you have an inherent affinity for. Send a disorganized employee to time management training, and she'll come back a mediocre time manager at best. Send an orderly employee instead, and he'll come back a time management pro who can specialize in keeping the whole company punctual. Take an auto mechanics class to learn to like cars, and you'll probably feel a little more self-sufficient but mostly weary. Take courses in areas you're really into, and you'll feel much more victorious.

By becoming better at what you're already good at rather than pushing yourself to take on what isn't your bailiwick, you can be more effective in life with less effort. Life is easier when you focus on your talents because you're at your best when you're doing what comes naturally. Letting go of what goes against your grain also frees up time and energy necessary to navigate through the constant disruptions and distractions of our fast-paced society. Paring your life down to your strong suits is a sure way to reduce the many options vying for your attention and help you feel more calm, clear, and centered amid the storm. When you focus on working and living in line with your organic interests and leanings, you will ultimately be in better condition to face disappointments, losses, mistakes, and other inevitable life adjustments that can't be avoided.

Before you get started on clarifying what strengths you may want to cultivate, it's important to keep in mind some parameters for living a strengths-based life. The pointers below will help you to consider more carefully what your talents are and how you can adapt them to make life at home and work more agreeable.

First, being exceptional at something doesn't mean you have to do it. Maybe you're a whiz at math but the last thing you want to do is your own taxes, much less work with numbers for a living. Perhaps you have a real green thumb but you can't stand yard work. You could have a genuine way with children but no desire to be a parent. Or maybe you're a gifted illustrator but know that transforming illustrating from a hobby into your life's work would take the joy out of it. Tapping into your strengths will make your life better only if your gut concurs that you should give those strengths more attention.

Second, putting your strengths at the center doesn't necessarily have to involve rearranging your whole life. If you determine after some soul searching that your particular talents make you suited for a different line of work, take your time thinking about what you might want to do next. There's no need to rush. For now, as you continue to make your way through this book, start with small changes that make a difference.

Remember Dan, the self-employed guy you met at the beginning of the book? He came to me for coaching because he was inundated with ideas for marketing his business and he wasn't sure where to go with them. I asked him what option for attracting customers—ranging from producing promotional pieces and articles to networking online and at professional conferences—sounded easiest to him. "Taking contacts to lunch and talking one on one," he said, and just like that we nailed the strength that could make his job less stressful and more rewarding.

Conventional wisdom had told Dan that targeting prospects individually was inefficient in comparison to reaching large numbers of people simultaneously through large social events and online forums. But he quickly realized that he could probably win more people over in the context he feels most comfortable in, and so he decided to stop spending long hours writing and chatting on the computer—activities he didn't really care for and is just okay at—and set a goal to take two contacts to lunch per week. That one small tweak helped to turn Dan and his business around.

Third, along with focusing on the strengths you *want* to develop and trying small changes to make a difference first, try not to let gender stereotypes and other preconceived notions get in your way as you carve out a strengths-based existence. Many of the couples who come to me for therapy complain that "I'm tired of doing all the budgeting," "She never helps me with the housework," or "Why should I have to make all the meals?" When I suggest to these couples that they divide household responsibilities according to talent— she agrees to handle the checkbook because she has a knack for finances, he agrees to do the cooking because he's a natural in the kitchen—life always gets better.

One final detail to keep in mind as you begin to take a strengths-based approach in life is that you don't have to throw out everything for which you don't have a talent. If you're drawn to something, even if you know full well it will never take you anywhere in life, by all means stick with it, but in a way that brings you enjoyment.

I love watching tennis tournaments, and one of the most satisfying sensations I know is hitting a tennis ball right at the sweet spot. I don't have a lick of talent for my favorite sport, however, yet one of my favorite summer activities is getting out in the fresh air and volleying a tennis ball back and forth. I don't take the sport seriously at all, so I don't put money or time into shopping for fancy tennis equipment or taking lessons to improve my serve. I also don't play with competitive tennis players who get easily frustrated with me on the court.

Likewise, I am fascinated by knitting. I love selecting fine wools and the meditative process of my knitting needles clicking together again and again. As much as I admire my supremely talented knitting friends who practically create their own multipatterned sweaters in their sleep, I stick with making scarves because any knitting more complicated than that just overwhelms me. The secret is to put your time and attention into the strengths that become increasingly invigorating as you take them further, find creative ways to take pleasure in the activities you love but aren't so good at, and do your best to drop the rest.

Apply the Wisdom

- Is there something you do that feels like a snap or a breeze, something that people compliment you on that you shrug off as "nothing," something you do well that you don't take seriously because it seems too easy? Whatever you come up with, anything from a knack for selecting nice gifts for people to an ease with electronic equipment, these are undoubtedly strengths that, if you feel inclined to recognize them as such, could be used to make your life easier. Contemplate ways you might further these strengths to be more successful.

- Think back to a professional or personal instance when you were really in the flow, so immersed in what you were doing that you didn't even sense time passing. You may have been working on a project, solving a problem, playing a game as a kid, using your hands, taking a walk, listening to music, shopping, driving, anything at all. Recall what you were doing, who was there with you, how you felt, any detail that makes the recollection more vivid. Consider that you were feeling so good during that instance because you were using your strengths. Now identify the strengths that come shining through in your example.

- Ask a sampling of people who know you well—friends, relatives, and colleagues—to identify your three top talents. Use their lists to pinpoint talents you might want to refine.

- Make a list of all the jobs you've ever had—paid jobs, volunteer jobs, chores around the house—and pull out the strengths you used in each. Get a piece of paper, and list all the strengths you come up with. Cross out the ones you don't want to develop any further. Focus on your remaining strengths, and ask yourself: How can I apply these strengths to make my life more enjoyable?

- Ask yourself frankly if any of your current interests and goals are causing you stress because your strengths don't lie in those areas. Letting go of some of those pursuits may allow you to redirect your resources to more promising ventures. Or, if you're really interested in something that isn't a strength—like maybe dancing for fitness despite a lack of coordination or enjoying your writing group for the social aspect despite a lack of writing talent—maybe reducing your expectations in those areas will bring you relief.

{ chapter 9 }
Operate with Optimism

My regular running route goes down a fairly unremarkable small town road. Average looking houses and yards, most of them kept up reasonably well, nothing striking or memorable. Except for one house that stands out and always intrigues and inspires me. Not because it is elaborate or grand in its architecture or grounds. To the contrary, this nondescript gray-shingled house is one of the humblest abodes in the neighborhood. What sets it a part and draws me in, quite simply, is its warm, unassuming, and soothing air of positivity.

In objective terms, this house isn't very attractive. Frankly, it's quite tiny, too close to the busy road, and not very private without a fence. Most people wouldn't want to live there because they'd feel constricted by its small size, unimpressed with its bland appearance, and annoyed with the near constant sound of traffic whizzing by. Were this house to go up for sale, it might appeal to a young couple as a makeshift "starter home" for a year or two, a place to wait while savings accrue for a loftier dream home.

I have never met the woman who lives in this house, but I am sure that she cares for her home deeply and sees it as a place to be cherished and made the most of, not as quarters that "will do" until money comes along for a more impressive dwelling. I know I am right because I have seen this woman working in her yard in the summer, lovingly tending to her robust garden of colorful wildflowers and ripening vegetables. And throughout the seasons I have noticed her gently placed affectionate touches. A couple of vibrant potted mums on her small front porch in autumn. A creatively carved pumpkin at the end of her driveway for Halloween. A carefully stacked pile of fireplace wood at the side of the house as the weather turns colder. Soft twinkling white lights around her small picture window and a fresh pine wreath on the front door at Christmas time.

Though it appears from the modest compact car in her driveway that this woman, somewhere in her forties or fifties, lives alone, another thing I'm sure of is that she is not lonely. I can tell by the out-of-state license plates on various cars in her little yard that she has a nice stream of weekend visitors. Sometimes when I run on summer mornings I catch glimpses of her and her weekend guests mingling in her small screen porch on the side of the house, laughing and talking and reaching for breakfast that she has laid out buffet style on a table. Every so often I see her wave from her front doorway to a visiting couple, wishing them a fun day of sightseeing as they emerge from her house and walk to their car, maps in hand. When I'm running by her house again on my way back home those mornings, I often see her strolling leisurely around her yard wearing a wide-brimmed straw hat and carrying a watering can, as if she is drinking in the beauty of her surroundings, unaware of the noisy cars (and nosey runner neighbor) passing by, noticing what's new and wonderful in her yard, and contemplating what she will do with her luscious day ahead.

What is so compelling about this woman is that she seems to have very little materially but nonetheless appears more than content with her lot in life. From what I can tell, she is a genuine "half glass full" person who is practiced in the art of honing in on what she has and not getting mired in what's wrong or missing. I envision her greeting every morning as a brand new opportunity to start fresh, no matter what has transpired the day before or what lies ahead. I imagine her beginning each day by asking, "What internal and external resources are available to me, and how can I make the most of these gifts to make this day as good as it can be?"

That capacity to look at life squarely, acknowledge what you're dealing with, and make it your mission to work with, rather than resist or regret, whatever situation is before you is optimism in its finest form. Optimism is not about denying reality, telling yourself everything is fine when it's not, pushing down uncomfortable emotions, or plastering a round-the-clock smile on your face.

Optimism is literally optimizing your options, which amounts to taking in the whole truth and choosing to focus on what's good about it. The experienced optimist knows that putting a positive spin on life, no matter what the circumstances, in no way brings immunity from curveballs. There's no getting through life as a human being without disappointments, failures, losses, and all sorts of other obstacles and unexpected disasters, but a positive attitude certainly makes the trials and tribulations of life easier to bear.

As a seasoned psychologist, I can say without reservation that optimism is a key quality necessary for moving successfully through life and work. Optimists are able to recover from setbacks, ignore naysayers, extract themselves from irreversible toxic situations, keep their eyes on the goal, and accomplish what's most meaningful to them. They're above the rest, every time.

And yet.

In our society of quick fixes, optimism is losing respect because it has been diluted to a superficial, speedy antidote for whatever ails you. Self-help books tell us that we can avoid the inevitable pain of being human by drowning out the negative with positive affirmations: *I can do whatever I want. I deserve the best. I am unstoppable (even if I have glaring issues and don't like myself very much).* Celebrities with chronic diseases tell us that we can avoid suffering by just "deciding" to be happy. Motivational speakers assure us that we can accomplish whatever we want by simply going over and over our desired positive outcomes in our heads. What we take away from all this "positive thinking" hype is that force-feeding ourselves happy thoughts will bulldoze us over insecurity, doubt, fear, sadness, grief, and every other inconvenient psychological experience and toward eternal bliss—faster than a bullet train.

If only optimism were so easy.

The thing about optimism is that it usually doesn't work instantly. You acquire a genuinely optimistic viewpoint little by little, as you would any other enviable skill. Optimism is a mature perspective that you strive for day after day, picking yourself up time and time again as you are tested by unanticipated events and get swept into negativity despite your best efforts. Eventually you develop a generally positive outlook that makes life easier than it would be otherwise. But optimism never makes your life pain free.

The hardest—and most crucial—part about being an optimist is trusting that if you let your emotions in—all of them, not just the appealing ones—you will bounce back to feeling good about yourself and the world. Authentic optimism demands your ability to stop and address grief, anger, uncertainty, dread, confusion, and other unsettling human feelings as they arise so that you can work through them, release the heaviness, and get back to the bright side. Optimists know that if unpleasant feelings are shoved down or ignored, they will find more dramatic ways—such as nightmares, irritability, or physical symptoms, for example, to get your attention. Like the tortoise that eventually beat the hare, optimists know that taking time out emotionally to recover from setbacks ultimately leads to greater resilience, peace of mind, and other rewards.

Optimists work hard at being optimists because they have learned that a realistic, appreciative, solution-focused mind-set is magnetic to resonant experiences and opportunities. Have you noticed that people who complain incessantly, blame everyone but themselves for their troubles, and seem to be forever in crisis just bring on more of the same? That's because negativity only attracts negativity. The bottom line is that good fortune comes much more readily to determined optimists who remain open to it.

Take my inspiring neighbor, for instance. I don't know her personal circumstances, but let's imagine that she has a low-paying job and can't afford a bigger home on a quieter street. If that's her scenario, her options are pretty clear-cut. She can resent that she lives in a small house near noisy traffic and spend her time griping and getting down on herself, longing for the day when her life will turn around. Or she can do what she's doing: make the very best of her circumstances, see the opportunities in her current situation, and live as fully as she can with what she has at hand. Either way, time will go by. But by choosing the latter, more positive approach, she will be able to look back at this period in her life proudly, recalling that her positive attitude made her time in that house better. And, more than likely, she'll also be able to look back and recount several ways that her optimism led to unanticipated opportunities.

The primary benefit of making the most of things is that whatever your goals—acing a job interview, making new friends, resolving the dilemmas you're dealt—you will be more likely to accomplish them with a perspective that by and large invites constructive circumstances. By choosing optimism over draining negativity, you create situations for yourself such as a safe and nurturing home environment out of wherever you've landed, for instance, that encourage your intuition to rise up and deliver insights that will lead to increasingly greater contentment. And of course one final benefit of making the most of what you have is that you end up with a clear, disciplined focus amid the clatter of our distracted, improvement-obsessed culture.

Apply the Wisdom

- Think of the people in your life or in books and movies that you admire most. Would you classify these people as optimists or pessimists? Why or why not? And what can you learn from these people as you contemplate living more optimistically.

- Consider how you might improve your home and work situations simply by being more optimistic. Are you really using your inner and external resources as best you can to make home and work the best possible? Think of one or two small changes you can make, from cleaning up your house to putting a plant on your desk at work, to get more out of your existing circumstances.

- Think of a problem you're dealing with currently, something you're really struggling with. Ask yourself what's perfect about this trying situation. Maybe a difficult person is helping you to become more patient. Perhaps unemployment is allowing you extra time to learn more about yourself. Consider how looking for the positive can improve your outlook and lead to creative solutions.

- Try looking at the bright side of things as much as you can for a few days and see what happens. Do you sense your mind opening up? Do you notice anything becoming easier? Are ideas and insights coming more readily? What are you attracting? Notice the impact your optimism has on how your life plays out.

{ chapter 10 }
Address Your Issues

Diana, a 44-year-old, stay-at-home-mom, is always running behind and missing appointments because her schedule is overflowing. Every day is like the day before Christmas as she runs last minute errands, rushes time-sensitive mail to the post office, and races to the bank just before closing to deposit money so her checks won't bounce. Diana is so preoccupied with so much to do that she can't find time to clean her house, often forgets to return important phone calls, and frequently annoys her friends by showing up late—or not at all—for social functions. Diana has good intentions and wants to be more reliable, but she can't seem to reduce her stress level and get her act together.

As you consider Diana's plight, I'm sure you can relate. If you take into account all the distractions and interruptions we face in this age of overwhelm, Diana doesn't seem so unusual, right? Sure she's overly frazzled and disorganized, but who isn't these days? Give the woman a break!

What makes Diana an unusual character in this book, however, is that she's not living in the present. Diana is actually the mother of one of my childhood friends, and the above description of her comes from my memory of her in the mid-seventies, when people generally weren't nearly as overwhelmed as they are now.

What I recall about Diana from spending significant time in her home is that her perennial state of stress was not caused by pervasive external factors. Like many of the women in my childhood neighborhood, she stayed home to raise her kids while her husband, a nice man and decent provider, worked. Diana and her family lived in a modest split-level ranch in a middle class suburb, with two cars, a stereo, and one television with three stations. No home in the neighborhood had (or had even heard of for that matter) a personal computer, cell phone, answering machine, fax machine, or microwave. Snail mail was something to get excited about because it was rarely junk; and important information sources were limited to the daily newspaper, the nightly news, and the neighborhood gossip. People didn't say things like, "I've been crazy busy" and "I've been working 24-7" because, unless they were one of those exceptionally ambitious "Type A" people, they were usually where they wanted to be on their to-do lists. Diana stood out like a sore thumb back then because overwhelm was not the communal, everyday experience it is today. Diana was unfocused for reasons unique to her, not because she was trying to keep up in a "crazy busy" world.

I bring up Diana to make an important point. Sometimes it's not the constant change, the pressure to improve, the never-ending swirl of options, or the ever-expanding repertoire of technological gadgets before you that are to blame for your distraction. Sometimes the culprit is something deeper; something that would be there even without the clamor.

At this stage in the book, as you begin to consider ways you can become more calm and directed in a culture that is always pushing you to do and be and have more, it's important to tease out personal factors that may be intensifying the life challenges you encounter.

As you might expect, almost every adult who enters my office these days is in search of stress relief. Most men and women want to work on being more balanced, feeling less hurried, getting more done with less pressure, accomplishing more in less time. Now and then I'll meet a client who just needs to learn to apply some of the lessons you've read about in previous chapters to make contemporary life more manageable. But more often than not, what my clients discover after a session or two is that underlying circumstances are exacerbating the sense of overwhelm our fast-paced culture creates. And in those cases, dealing with the underlying circumstances is an unavoidable *but hugely worthwhile* prerequisite to stress relief.

Take Nick, Jill, and Olivia for example. At their first sessions with me each described a longstanding, exhausting sense of never being finished or accomplished. On the surface, these three professional adults seemed to be understandably worn out from the do it all, have it all, be it all push of modern culture. But individually, in terms of their very distinct histories behind the stress, Nick, Jill, and Olivia had varying concerns that would likely continue to create stress, even in the face of the most sophisticated stress-reduction techniques, until they were reckoned with.

Nick, raised by extremely demanding parents, realized that he was worn out from trying futilely for most of his life to do something that would finally make his parents proud. But nothing—getting the most home runs in Little League, making high school high honor roll, earning an Ivy League scholarship, or even winning a major election—had ever been good enough to earn their validation. Letting go of the need for approval from his parents and learning to set his own standards for success is what helped Nick.

Jill, a partner at a graphic design firm, discovered that her fatigue was associated with an ingrained belief that she had to be nice to everyone to be liked. She had become so accommodating at work, always offering to stay late and on weekends and to work at home to make sure team deadlines got met, that she had virtually no personal life. The only answer for Jill was to learn to set firm limits with her staff and trust that people would like her—in fact, trust that they would probably like her *more*—if she didn't bend over backwards to enable them.

Olivia, a freelance writer in her fifties, learned that contentment was always at bay because she didn't feel deserving of happiness. She had been burdened by tremendous guilt since college graduation when she decided to accept a journalism position in New York rather than return home to Iowa to help her siblings nurse their dying mother. Once Olivia saw through therapy that her mother probably wanted her to pursue her career, she was able to let go and allow herself to enjoy her success.

These are just three instances of how distinct individual issues can be implicated in the common experience of strain and tension. And of course, there are many more examples I could give you. People are held back by all sorts of unsettling internal experiences, ranging from irrational worries and doubts to festering bitterness and rage. It's not a question of whether or not you have issues, because frankly we all have issues. It's more a question of whether you have particular issues that are making your life overly complicated.

So how do you know if there's something you should take a deeper look at?

It's tricky to distinguish between normal, everyday stress and signs of a fundamental internal condition because the manifestations can be so similar. The circumstances below can lead to distraction, weariness, irritability, disturbed sleep, inattention, impulsivity, anxiety, indecision, disorganization, feeling scared, feeling hopeless and helpless, and other symptoms that are often chalked up to overwhelm:

- A significant loss that you haven't fully grieved
- A regret or mistake that you haven't forgiven yourself for
- Unresolved anger or resentment
- Ingrained beliefs that create impossible expectations, such as: I have to be perfect to be okay, everyone must like me or I'm a loser, I have to make everyone happy, I must accomplish huge goals to be worthy
- Inherent attention, organizational, and/or impulse control deficits (i.e., attention deficit disorder (ADD))
- Clinical anxiety
- Clinical depression
- Learning disorders

- Substance abuse
- Fear of intimacy/extreme difficulty trusting others
- Trauma from which you haven't recovered
- Anything from your past that still haunts you
- Anything about your future that brings on dread

Before you decide that one of the above conditions may be causing havoc in your life, keep in mind that you can rule something out if it isn't getting in your way. There are as many psychological theories as there are psychologists, but one thing most of us agree on is that an issue needs addressing if it's interfering with your ability to effectively participate in the basic responsibilities of adulthood. If your thoughts and moods are negatively impacting your work, relationships with others, or relationship with yourself, then you may want to seek out a professional. On the other hand, if the only internal roadblock you can think of is an intense snake phobia and you live in Manhattan, it's probably okay to not seek treatment.

Something else psychologists agree on is that important lessons not reckoned with will circle back, often in sneaky, unrelenting ways, until they get your attention. Freud was the first to put forth the basic tenet of psychological health, that if you accomplish the tasks of the developmental stage you're in, be it toilet training, learning the alphabet, surviving social rejection, or leaving the nest, you will be fully equipped for the next stage. And if you fail to master the tasks of a particular stage, you move forward unable to handle the increasingly complex challenges of life. Whatever you don't work out, in other words, you take with you to your next destination, and that's where psychological baggage comes from. So if there's some unfinished business from your past that's weighing on you, it makes sense to take time out to learn what you didn't get right the first time.

One more narrowing down rule psychologists see eye to eye on is that an issue is most likely an issue if it is part of a destructive pattern in your life. If you've noticed, for example, that you always seem to become romantically involved with partners who cheat on you, that you seem to get fired more than most people you know, or that your family and friends complain to you about a particular habit or trait, then there is most likely some inner matter making trouble for you.

If you determine after some soul searching that you do have issues that need addressing, please be patient with yourself. If an issue is powerful enough to thwart your progress in life, it most likely didn't build up overnight, is quite stubborn, and may take a while to deal with. Yes, sometimes it's possible to free yourself from psychological baggage by doing something as simple as writing a letter of apology or having a good cry, but getting to the root of an issue, working through it, letting it go, and moving forward usually requires persistence and practice. Especially in a culture that discourages slowing down and looking inward for direction, it can be tough to swallow that if you do have an issue blocking your way, you may have to take some time out to tend to it. What's important to remember is that you have control over your individual issues, and dealing with them will lead to an enhanced capacity to cope with information overload, non-stop change, and other aspects of life over which you *don't* have control.

Apply the Wisdom

- On a scale of one to ten, with one being the least and ten being the most, pinpoint your average stress level. Now ask yourself honestly: is there some personal issue that is contributing to your stress level? And, if so, what would your stress level likely be if you didn't have that personal issue?

- Draw a long horizontal line on a large piece of paper and divide it into five-year periods of your life. For each five-year period, identify the biggest challenge you faced. Then look over your time line and consider whether those challenges have truly been reckoned with. If you decide that you have some unfinished work to do, explore some small steps you might take to do that work. If you realize that you want to forgive someone, maybe you can look for a good book on forgiveness. If you decide you never really learned how to be in a solid romantic relationship, perhaps you want to talk to a friend whose relationship you admire.

- Ask a close friend or family member, someone you can rely on to be supportive, trustworthy, sensitive, and truthful, if they can think of any personal issues you may want to work on. Take the feedback you hear seriously and consider small steps you can take to improve in that area.

- Ask yourself candidly if it's possible that you may be hanging on to a particular issue because it is serving you in some way. Perhaps being unable to let go of a past romance could be protecting you from taking a chance in a new relationship. Maybe you procrastinate because you're afraid that you won't succeed if you give something your best, most organized shot. If you determine that your issues are defending you against risk in some way, entertain the possibility that working through those issues might lead to some positive outcomes, like falling in love with the right person next time or finding out that you really do have what it takes to accomplish whatever you've been putting off.

- If you think you may need professional guidance to address your issue or issues, consider setting up an appointment with your primary care physician, clergyperson, or a therapist for counsel.

{ chapter 11 }
Boost Your Emotional Intelligence

As you might imagine, I am a lover of self-help books. Always looking for ways to learn and grow personally and professionally and help others do the same, I am drawn to books that invigorate me with innovative ideas for handling the challenges of life and work. Having read literally hundreds of self-help books since I caught the bug in early adolescence, I can advise people on the best books to read for whatever human conundrum ails them. An armful of self-help books—*Think and Grow Rich* by Napoleon Hill, *Man's Search For Meaning* by Victor Frankel, *The Power of Positive Thinking* by Norman Vincent Peale, to name a few—stay with me as classic companions I can go to again and again for timeless wisdom and inspiration. But if I could recommend just one book for summing up the secret to success at home and work, it wouldn't be a whole book; it would be just one chapter of a book, and one incredibly profound sentence in particular that I'd steer people toward.

The book I am speaking of is *A Handy Guide to Grown-Ups,* written in 1950 by an 11-year-old American girl named Jennifer Owsley. Random House agreed to publish this book only after taking exhaustive measures to ensure that the implausibly astute advice it offered—one of Jennifer's gems is that "The essential difference between adults and children is that adults are more polite than they are honest and children are more honest than they are polite" — was written by a child. This book has been out of print for many years, and I stumbled upon a worn copy by chance at a yard sale. Designed for children, the slim, illustrated volume is a breezy read. Which is why when I sat down with a glass of iced tea to read it one hot summer day a couple of years ago, I wasn't expecting to find the secret to success summed up in one kid-friendly sentence.

The critical chapter is a primer on the various personality types of schoolteachers—the burnt out spinster and the inexperienced newbie, for example—and how to address their assorted quirks. Jennifer offers customized advice for each. To get along with the mean-spirited teacher, you do this. To get along with the overly controlling teacher, you do that. And then Jennifer concludes the chapter with this unassuming pivotal sentence: *The best teachers are the ones you don't have to worry about getting along with because they know how to get along with you.*

Therein is one of the best recommendations I could ever give anyone for making life and work as smooth a sail as possible.

Know how to get along with people.

That's it.

My guess is that the extraordinary insight of that one sentence I find so riveting wasn't recognized as such when it was written in 1950. That's because in those days success in work and life was thought to be intricately linked to IQ or intelligence quotient, a measure of cognitive capacity. The assumption was that if you were beyond your peers in terms of your ability to memorize and apply facts and figures, you were destined to advance in school, at the office, and throughout life. The higher your IQ, the more likely it was that you'd be happy, healthy, and wealthy.

But the emergence of Positive Psychology, a relatively new domain of psychology concerned with the qualities that allow people to excel and thrive, has brought about the realization that the recipe for conventional success goes far beyond being book smart. No matter how enormous the fund of information in your head, how flawless your record of acing exams, or how uncanny your ability to navigate even the most complicated problems on paper, a high IQ alone won't cut it. Sometimes, in fact, an off-the-charts IQ can actually *hinder* success.

It's pretty common wisdom among psychologists these days that you're more likely to be successful if you are adept at building and sustaining positive relationships—not only with others but with yourself. Consider the professor who can quote any work of fiction but is beyond the pale arrogant and doesn't know how to converse with her secretary let alone relate to people outside her ivory tower. Or think about the virtuoso engineer who can envision solutions to just about any mechanical quandary but doesn't know how to hold his short temper or gain assistance from a customer service person. These are both stereotypes of supposedly intellectually gifted people who are clueless when it comes to actual "people skills," but you get the point. Unless you are so incredibly talented (the unbearably demanding actor, for instance, who is a box office magnet; or the insensitive physician who is tolerated for his proficiency with diagnosing despite his lack of bedside manner), brilliance alone won't get you very far if you don't know how to conduct yourself appropriately in everyday social situations.

Over the past 20 years or so, the term *Emotional Intelligence* has been used increasingly to describe what is now considered key to personal and professional accomplishment. In a world where almost any piece of data can be obtained with a quick Google search, advanced knowledge is no longer a hot commodity limited to scholars, savants, and specialists. As information becomes more and more available to the masses, a high IQ isn't enough to make you stand out. Emotional intelligence—your capacity for understanding and managing yourself and understanding and managing your relationships with others—is now the central factor used to predict achievement.

What emotional intelligence amounts to is being simultaneously tuned into yourself and other people. Being tuned into yourself means having an accurate read on your strengths and limitations; understanding what you are feeling and how your feelings affect you; and being able to regulate your emotions, thinking, and behavior to get your needs met and accomplish your goals. Being tuned into others means being attentive and open to the feelings and perspectives of those you encounter, being mindful of how you impact the people around you, and being able to adapt your own behavior—without sacrificing your safety or values—to better communicate, cooperate, and collaborate with others. In essence, you are emotionally intelligent if you take responsibility for knowing, handling, protecting, and motivating yourself in ways that at least don't interfere with the rights or comfort of others and at best inspire and encourage others.

One of the first things I learned as a psychologist is that people with the most capacity for emotional intelligence are most apt to seek mental health treatment. After all, a big part of emotional intelligence is being open to personal change and adaptation. Early in my training I volunteered on the psychiatric ward of a Chicago hospital. My job was to check visitors in to see friends and family members who'd been hospitalized. Though many of the visitors were perfectly nice, reasonable people, a good portion of them were difficult in some way. In some cases, and I'm not joking here, some of the visitors were crazier than the people who were locked up! Fifteen or so years later, I realize that it's often emotionally unintelligent people who drive others, usually more emotionally intelligent people who find their emotionally unintelligent family members, friends, bosses, and co-workers literally crazy-making, to psychological collapse.

Because seriously emotionally unintelligent people have a poor capacity for personal change, it is up to others to get along with them. To the emotionally intelligent person, "getting along" ranges from interacting with those who annoy you without letting them get under your skin to limiting or ending contact with people who are downright toxic, abusive, or otherwise impossible to deal with. Much of the work I do is about helping responsible adults increase their emotional intelligence by learning how to rise above the exasperating people in their lives. In other words, setting appropriate limits and boundaries when necessary so that they don't have to get dragged into unproductive arguments or game playing or go around walking on eggshells.

Along with knowing how to deal effectively with thorny personalities, emotionally intelligent people are nicely equipped to meet the daily challenges we all encounter in our time-pressed, fast-paced culture. Because emotionally intelligent people take responsibility for managing their feelings and their relationships, they know how to step back, get perspective, and do what is necessary to be productive under pressure and amid distraction. Because emotionally intelligent people are conscious of themselves and others, they are proactive in preventing personal and social issues from flaring up. They make it a point to face inner and outer conflict as it arises, and so they are minimally burdened by baggage associated with denying personal problems and avoiding confrontation.

What emotional intelligence comes down to is changing your personality and relational skills to compensate for the people and situations you have no power over. Being emotionally intelligent means looking within and asking: How can I adjust myself within reason to make my life easier? Sometimes the answer is acknowledging and addressing your emotional weak points, like resisting an urge to be impulsive and learning to calm down instead of lashing out when you're angry, or getting into the habit of processing pain with a therapist rather than giving in to your tendency to repress emotional distress. Other times the answer can be acknowledging and overcoming a personality blind spot, like fear of change in a world where change is constant or difficulty sitting still and listening when your role as a parent requires that. The answer could also be anticipating and addressing the needs of the significant people in your life, like knowing that your boss will be better able to focus on an important meeting with you if you enter her office with her favorite coffee drink in hand or understanding that addressing a conflict with your spouse will go much better over a leisurely weekend dinner than when you're both rushing out the door to work in the morning.

What emotional intelligence *is not* is twisting yourself into contortions or ingratiating yourself with others to force an outcome you want. Chances are you've been turned off by a salesperson who you know is saying your name over and over again not because she is tuned into you but because she has learned in some seminar that repeating your name will encourage you to trust her and subsequently buy her product. You've probably also experienced the overzealous waitperson who mechanically kneels at your table to make eye contact with you, and inserts himself into your private conversation to build rapport with you because he has been programmed to perform these gestures to create instant intimacy. Unlike these cloying instances where people you hardly know forge inappropriate connections to extract money from your pocket, a truly emotionally intelligent person takes an interest in you in ways that make you feel genuinely respected and comfortable—and they do it without compromising their own integrity.

Being emotionally intelligent doesn't mean that you have to turn yourself into an extroverted social butterfly if you're a shy, retiring type. What emotional intelligence does mean is having the basic social sense necessary to realize that if you're stranded at the airport, you have a far better chance of getting a free hotel room for the night if you empathize with your harried ticket agent rather than scream at her and stomp your feet. It also means having the wisdom to know when anticipating and addressing the needs of others has become exhausting and draining and it's time to draw the line. Emotionally intelligent people are able to get along with others—without losing themselves.

Think of it this way: Whether you feel completely at ease behind the wheel of a car or find driving a necessary evil (as it is for me), you need to follow the rules of responsible driving—know how your car handles in varying weather and traffic conditions, and respect the other drivers on the road—to safely reach your destination. And it's the same with emotional intelligence. You could be an authentic "people person" or you could prefer solitude to human interaction. Either way, you live in a social world, and so you need to know how to handle yourself and others in the varying, ever-changing cultural conditions that impact us all. Unless you show respect for yourself and other people, negotiating yourself in and around prickly interpersonal situations without putting yourself or others out, getting where you want to go in life can be as stressful as walking down an unfamiliar street blindfolded.

The bottom line is that enhancing your emotional intelligence is the most efficient way to enjoy your own company and engage the support and camaraderie of others. In an age where diversity is the norm, people who know how to get along with all sorts of people are the ones who can get through life with the least amount of stress and make the biggest impact. Especially as people grow increasingly more comfortable in front of a computer screen than in face-to-face human interactions, knowing how to manage yourself to effectively engage others is not just a handy skill, it's a fine and rare art worth pursuing.

Apply the Wisdom

- A big part of emotional intelligence is seeing yourself as others see you. Ask yourself honestly if you have an informed read on your strengths and limitations. Then ask a few people you trust and respect what your blind spots are (we *all* have blind spots), and consider whether it might make sense to work on improving yourself in these areas.

- Think about a person or situation you're having trouble with. Now, ask yourself if you have some responsibility for the problem. Maybe you are being overly judgmental, critical, or impatient and could stand to be more compassionate, encouraging, or tolerant to improve your circumstances. Decide on one aspect you have control over, vow to make a small change, and see what happens.

- Consider what sorts of people most push your buttons. Is it people who talk too much or too little who get on your nerves? Or is it people who are too laid back or too controlling that drive you up the wall? One sure way to increase your emotional intelligence is to learn how to deal better with the people you regard as most difficult. What small changes might you make in your next interactions with these people to make things easier? Remember that in some cases, when the difficult person you're dealing with is consistently draining you despite your emotionally intelligent maneuvers, your best bet is probably to cut ties entirely rather than waste more of your valuable energy.

- Think about the people you respect most. What aspects of emotional intelligence do these people most employ? Make a list of the qualities you might work on to become more emotionally intelligent yourself.

{ chapter 12 }
Have a Healthy Respect for Time

I felt relaxed, confident, and empowered like never before when I returned home to Chicago from my first trip overseas at age 26. The company I'd been working for had folded at the beginning of the summer and I'd been given a three-month severance package. What better thing for a young woman with no attachments to do than spontaneously take a trip to Europe? For four weeks I leisurely traipsed around fancying myself the star of a good road movie, shedding layer upon layer of established structure and convention as I became one with my nomadic adventure and allowed my natural rhythm to emerge.

Unfettered by schedules and responsible to no one but me, I easily immersed myself in the unhurried tempo of European life. I loved spending long, uninterrupted hours reading new authors on trains; writing and sketching in my journal a few times a day on beaches, in parks, and at outdoor cafés; enjoying rambling conversations and spur-of-the-moment adventures with fellow travelers I met along the way. I literally let my hair down, stopped wearing make-up, sometimes went days without showering, and mailed most of my clothes and toiletries back home after my first week upon realizing the benefits of traveling light. My carefree mood in Europe quickly helped me to see the ridiculousness of rushing around like Americans do, and I was determined not to fall back into that frantic pace. I had discovered the peace of mind that comes from living according to my internal clock, and I was going to bring this enlightened perspective home with me.

I remember feeling quite elevated those first few weeks back, mentally rolling my eyes at all the people in suits carrying briefcases and walking briskly, their tight, serious faces showing clear signs of stress and strain. I wanted to stop these people, shake them, and ask what the hurry was and why they couldn't slow down, take their constricting suits off, and *just be*.

But naturally, as a single woman with a dwindling bank account, I couldn't maintain my haughty European perspective for long. Pretty soon I was pounding pavement looking for my next job. Then I started working again, and before I knew it I was back to my ambitious old self, competing for recognition, all zipped up in my business attire, catching commuter trains, meeting deadlines, and setting and accomplishing alluring goals. I'd been idealistic, I realized. As long as I was going to participate in the American workforce, I'd have to live according to imposed standards and schedules that would create pressure, and I'd have to do my best to manage my time like everyone else not privileged by independent wealth.

A few years later I was at a professional conference in the heart of New York City, and I'd volunteered to go out and get lunch for my colleagues. I remember weaving myself through a massive current of hurrying people, carrying a bagful of those mile high deli sandwiches New York is famous for when all of a sudden a man in a suit walked smack into me, knocking me to the ground and sending the sandwiches flying. I sat there on the sidewalk, incredulous, as the man and everyone else just kept right on walking as if nothing had happened. I could tell by the faraway, ultra-focused looks in their eyes that no one had stopped to help me because they *hadn't even noticed* me or my bag of sandwiches! As I picked myself and the sandwiches up, I laughed out loud at the absurdity of being so intent on getting somewhere quickly that you don't even see what's directly in your path.

And then it occurred me. My laid back European mind-set certainly isn't practical in a pervasively fast-paced country, but neither is it practical to be so absorbed in accomplishing things swiftly that there is no time left to be human.

Americans are a diverse lot of people. But one thing we have always had in common is a fierce investment in doing as much as possible within as little time as possible. This longstanding national trend toward efficiency has served us well in the form of innumerable inventions that have made life easier and sped real progress. Being able to transport ourselves and infinite products via trains, planes, and automobiles instead of horses and wagons has certainly enriched our lives and catapulted commerce beyond measure. Washers and driers, microwaves, and all sorts of other household appliances have rescued us from monotonous, unforgiving domestic labor. The telephone, TV, radio, and computer have paved the way for increasingly smooth and rapid communication. Cake mixes, frozen dinners, and other processed foods have allowed us to keep ourselves fueled much more easily than when we had to make everything "from scratch." And ever-evolving medical procedures and medicines have helped to hasten recovery from countless diseases and medical conditions.

But the ironic thing about a nation hell-bent on saving time—and the problem with our addiction to efficiency— is that the more time-saving devices and systems we have available, the less time we seem to have at our disposal. The twisted logic is that whatever time is freed up should be devoted to more fast-paced activities, so we rarely get to experience the spare time these time-saving solutions were initially meant to create. Instead of reading a frivolous novel while our clothes are drying, we should clean the kitchen or work in the garden. Rather than take a much-needed nap on our business flight, we should read a professional journal or catch up on paperwork via our laptop. As time-saving solutions become more advanced, our deadlines become shorter and our standards more competitive. In the apt words of a former workaholic boss of mine, "When I'm not using extra time to accomplish more work, I feel like I'm throwing away time—and money."

Most of us realize that something must be terribly off kilter when the impact of increasingly sophisticated time-saving solutions is an escalating sense that time is running out. What we've done in response is to "manage" our time better, which means trying to stretch, expand, crunch, and otherwise manipulate time to reclaim a sense of control. Americans spend millions of dollars annually on time management books, conferences, coaching, and workshops, but no matter how many time management tactics we try, we just can't seem to achieve a sense of accomplishment or mastery when it comes to our schedules.

What's beginning to dawn on us is that the time management approach—wrestling with time to surpass the limitations it imposes, sometimes to the point where we compromise our health and happiness—is all wrong. No matter what we do, there will always be just 24 hours in a day, we will always need an average of eight hours of sleep per night, we will always recover from intense periods of applying ourselves only by breaking away to replenish and restore our inner resources, and we will each have (on average) about 75 years before we expire.

The secret to feeling less time-pressed is to give up on managing time and start managing ourselves *within* time.

Managing yourself within time involves two components:

1. Stepping back and considering all the time-saving options available.

2. Selecting only the options that allow you to simultaneously accomplish your goals efficiently, make room for experiences that can't and shouldn't be rushed, and encourage your own natural rhythm to unfold in the areas that are fulfilling to you.

To get an idea of how you might better manage yourself within time according to your unique situation, consider my clients Paul and Joe, a couple who came to me because they were feeling stressed despite their valiant efforts to use various well-intended short-cuts. To create time to enjoy each other on weeknights, they'd been reserving Sunday afternoons to make a week's worth of dinners at once so all they'd have to do was pop frozen entrees in the oven at the end of the workday. The problem was Paul considered cooking sheer drudgery and resented spending part of his weekend in the kitchen, and Joe, who enjoyed cooking, missed the ritual of unwinding at the end of the day by fixing inspired meals. Taking over the kitchen allowed Joe to enjoy his culinary passion every day, and Paul was able to wind down from work with activities Joe had no patience for, like reading sports magazines cover to cover and writing long, colorful emails to family and friends. This couple found that they were less stressed when they allowed each other to use time-saving strategies according to their individual tastes.

Holly, another client, learned to manage herself within time by taking a more reasonable approach to her high-pressure job. A public relations executive at a competitive firm, she'd been trying to outdo her colleagues by coming in early, leaving late, and eating lunch at her desk. Holly learned that she could actually accomplish more by working in 90-minute shifts interspersed with breaks for high-protein snacks, fresh air, and stretching. She also realized that she could be more alert and proficient by leaving the office at 5 o'clock and going to bed a little earlier. By respecting her need for recovery periods between intense sprints of thinking and writing, and getting more sleep at night, Holly ended up feeling more energized and producing better work.

For Patrick, who sought therapy to speed recovery from a painful break-up, managing himself within time meant giving in to his human need to deal with his feelings rather than pushing them down as a way to move on. By changing his view of grieving from a pesky interruption to a necessary part of rebuilding his life, he learned to value the time-consuming but essential process of working through emotional upheaval. Patrick also saw, by taking a sabbatical from his treadmill so that he could walk in nature as a way to process his feelings in solitude, that the insights he gained from clearing his head in the woods were worth the 15 minutes it took to drive to and from the trail he'd discovered. Having a treadmill in his living room no longer seemed like a clever convenience.

What Paul and Joe, Holly, and Patrick found from becoming more discerning about time-saving strategies is that efficiency serves us well only when we are saving time in ways that don't take us away from who we want to be. Being competent in the face of near constant change and distraction so that we can accomplish what's important to us requires that we put our time into the pursuits and pastimes that are essential to our personal character and sanity. Shortcuts enrich our lives when we use them to make room for what brings us meaning.

Apply the Wisdom

- How would you describe your relationship with time? Is it healthy, not healthy? Is time on your side, not on your side? How might an improved relationship with time impact your perspective?

- What are your favorite time-saving strategies? How do these strategies enhance your life?

- What time-saving strategies take away from your enjoyment of life? Consider whether tossing out these strategies and taking the scenic route might make your life more enjoyable and ultimately put you in a better frame of mind to deal with everyday pressures.

- How might you take time out to be ultimately more efficient at home and work?

- Have you suffered consequences from not taking the necessary time to work through difficult life experiences? If so, would it be helpful to process any emotions that may be slowing you down?

- What would you do if you had three extra hours per week to spend any way you want? How might you carve out time in your schedule to do just that?

{ chapter 13 }
Engage in Sensible Multitasking

Imagine that you're sitting in a restaurant booth enjoying lunch with a close friend you haven't seen in a while. You are deep in conversation with this cherished person, feeling extremely grateful to have this precious time together to catch up. You lean in closer as your friend begins to update you on a pressing personal problem, and just then you hear someone in the booth behind you mention the name of a colleague. You naturally want to keep listening to your friend, but you are now also invested in being alert to any intriguing details that might come from the conversation behind you. You try to split your attention evenly so as not to miss out on anything, but within a minute or so you feel too distracted to pay sufficient attention to either situation. You decide to let go of the conversation behind you in favor of being there for your friend. And your focus on the person across the table is quickly restored.

What this common situation illustrates is that it's not feasible to concurrently give your full attention to two activities each requiring it. Most of us have experienced such a moment or some variation on it: talking to someone at a party while also trying to make out the lyrics of a song playing in the background, or taking in the audio AND the visual of two separate movies on adjacent televisions on a store shelf. Most of us also know full well that when we dilute our focus like that, we pick up only fractured bits and pieces and don't integrate the whole of anything. That's why smart human beings go to the library to study for exams, turn off the radio when they're watching a complicated movie, and minimize interfering noise when they really want to hear what someone has to say.

So why is it then that despite having learned the undeniable limits of the delicate human attention span many times over, perfectly reasonable people persist in dividing their awareness between two or more activities requiring complete concentration? Why would a seemingly levelheaded adult routinely read and send text messages while driving, engage in serious cell phone conversation while walking down a busy city street, or work on a significant project via laptop while participating in a critical conference call? *Even when* widely and repeatedly publicized hard evidence, such as increased emergency room visits caused by texting behind the wheel of a fast-moving car and having a cell phone conversation while negotiating crowded urban streets on foot, shows us that this kind of senseless multitasking doesn't work?

Otherwise sensible people act in irrational ways because they want to believe, despite their better judgment, in the false promise of misguided yet popular cultural myths. Though we know better, it's easy to convince ourselves of what we wish were true, that technology saves time by making it possible to wholly engage in two exacting endeavors at once. We don't want to face the truth that technology isn't powerful enough to expand the limited capacity of the human attention span.

Cell phones, Blackberries, computers, and other technological devices are wonderful tools for making work and life more efficient, enjoyable, flexible, and manageable, but only if we use them judiciously. Judicious use means recognizing that if you use technology in ways that force you to put your full attention in two places at once, you are not saving time. To the contrary, you are wasting it.

Technology *will* save you time (and your sanity and quite possibly your life, for that matter) if you recognize the limits of the average adult brain. Combining two activities requiring your total attention means doing neither activity well. Many activities, of course, can be blended for greater efficiency without compromising performance. As long as you are applying technology in ways that don't distract you from situations that require your full focus, you are engaging in what I call sensible multitasking.

Here are some ideas for putting sensible multitasking into practice:

- Carry your laptop with you so you can read and respond to emails, work on projects, read your favorite blogs, and download music and books while you're waiting to board a flight, filling time left by a client who doesn't show up, or enduring other delays.

- Listen to music or a book on your iPod while you're driving, exercising, or cleaning the house.

- Participate in a conference call via cell phone while taking a walk somewhere peaceful and away from traffic.

- Enjoy casual phone conversation while you're doing the dishes.

- Fold laundry while you're watching TV.

- Read and respond to text messages while you're getting your hair cut or standing in the grocery store check-out line.

Now I realize that just reading this chapter won't be enough to convince you to abolish your senseless multitasking behavior. Temptations to disregard the logical reasons why it's impossible to accomplish two challenging tasks at once are everywhere and hard to resist. Even a savvy psychologist who knows more than most people do about what the brain can and can't do falls sometimes. Despite my education and experience, my need to believe that senseless multitasking works is strong and stubborn—because, after all, life would be oh so much easier if it did work, wouldn't it? Deluded by wishful thinking just like you, I sometimes can't resist reaching for my cell phone when I'm walking from the parking garage to my office in the morning or driving home in my car at night. Just like you, I find myself checking my email and surfing the internet during important conference calls. And just like you, I find it frighteningly easy to convince myself, on those occasions when I simply can't stop myself from dangerously combining two demanding activities in hope that I'll save time, that those senseless multitasking emergency room visits will only happen to "someone else."

In a culture that provocatively pushes the fantasy that the brain can do far more than it's capable of, the only way to give up useless multitasking is to make it hard to engage in. You can thwart your impulses to multitask senselessly by putting your cell phone and your Blackberry in the trunk of your car before you get behind the wheel or by shutting down and zipping up your laptop before you get on a conference call. As with any habit you are trying to acquire, you will fall off track and go back to your old ways from time to time, but you will eventually reach a point where the desire to engage in dangerous multitasking becomes less powerful.

What works best to dissuade me from recklessly splitting my attention is recalling the old-fashioned multitasking example from the beginning of this chapter. To bring myself back to my senses, I remember all my failed attempts to participate in a meaningful conversation while trying to pay close attention to something else. What strikes me is that every time I have tried to push my attention span beyond reasonable limits, I have gone from feeling calm, centered, and comfortable to feeling distracted, disengaged, and uneasy—within seconds. What also occurs to me about those times is that once I realize that I simply can't give my full attention to two important endeavors at once, it takes a little while to move back to that considerably more pleasant place of being present in an enjoyable moment. These two realizations remind me that dividing my attention and then pulling my attention back and redirecting it is a stressful process that almost makes my head hurt. Then I see clearly that pushing my brain uncomfortably beyond what it was built to do is only wearing me out, eroding my concentration capacity, and stealing enjoyment from my life. Once again, I comprehend that I will be in a much better position to thrive in a world of constant distractions if I do my best to treat my brain well.

Apply the Wisdom

- Try out one or two of my sensible multitasking suggestions and see how you do. Do you notice any positive effects?

- Go beyond my suggestions and come up with some of your own. How else might you combine two activities to accomplish your goals more efficiently—without putting impossible demands on your attention span?

- Consider the multitasking crimes you are most guilty of. Is it your cell phone, laptop, or Blackberry that tempts you most? Consider how you might change your behavior to keep temptation at bay, and experiment a little with the preventive actions you come up with.

- It is primarily the prospect of saving time that keeps us multitasking. What incentives can you think of for cutting down on senseless multitasking? Perhaps not using your cell phone while walking or driving to and from work will give you a daily opportunity to clear your head and allow your intuition to rise up with important insights. Not surfing the internet during phone conversations will allow you to improve your listening skills and become a more appealing conversationalist. Or delegating undivided time every day to thoughtfully responding to emails rather than answering them impulsively could help you to be a more effective communicator. What other positive results could come from exercising a singular focus more regularly?

- It's hard to practice sensible multitasking because, let's face it, technology can be pretty alluring. So that you don't feel deprived, try keeping yourself on a positive multitasking path by rewarding yourself for good multitasking behavior with technological treats. For example, give yourself an uninterrupted hour of internet surfing, download a favorite book or movie, or buy yourself ten iTunes in exchange for one week of no texting while driving.

{ chapter 14 }
Redefine Living in the Moment

Jeannette, a 41-year-old mother of three young children, is in such a hurry that she has come to my office on a cold winter day with her freshly washed hair soaking wet. Alex, a 46-year-old engineer, is 15 minutes late and out of breath as he sits down and announces that he must leave early for an unexpected meeting. Patty, a 37-year-old student and personal trainer, cuts me off twice during our session to answer her cell phone. Jeannette, Alex, and Patty are clients who have sought therapy for unrelated reasons. What brings them together in this paragraph is that all of them consistently have difficulty arriving on time for and staying focused during our sessions. And all three have told me more than once as they've sat on the couch across from me that what they need to feel better is to start "living in the moment."

I need to start living in the moment. If I had a dime for every time I've heard a wiped out, over-extended adult say that to me, I really would be the wealthiest psychologist this side of the Mississippi. This concept of living in the moment is a mirage, a panacea, an intangible goal that many adults long to achieve as the ultimate remedy to stress. Self-assured celebrities, cocky self-help book authors, high-priced life coaches, and enigmatic talk show hosts claim to be happy with their lives because they have accomplished this longed-for goal. They tell us that we can join them in their in-the-moment bliss if we just "be here now" and "breeeeeeeeeeeeeeeeeeathe." And so we continue our struggle to conquer this great feat of somehow stopping time—despite our jam-packed schedules—and just soak up the instant we're in, all the while feeling increasingly inept because we can't get it right, thus feeling ever more guilty and deprived because moments still seem to fly right by despite our best intentions to hold onto them and pin them down.

When my clients tell me they need to start living in the moment to reduce their stress, I ask them what living in the moment really means. Most of them have trouble answering the question because they haven't really ever thought about it. They just know they need to do it because they've been inundated with the media message that "living in the moment" is the answer to their problems. After a little reflection, they typically respond with something like, "Living in the moment means being able to block out my negative thoughts and appreciate what's going on right now," "It means being totally present where I am and feeling the joy, beauty, and possibility in and around me," or "It means slowing down my mind and becoming fully engaged with where I am, what I'm doing, and who I'm with."

What I say to clients in response to their "living in the moment" definitions is that they are setting impossible standards for themselves that are most likely exacerbating the stress they're experiencing. Is it really feasible, I ask them, to "live in the moment" in the ways they are describing, in the fastest paced country in the world, in a culture where we are chronically distracted, interrupted, and jostled; where we are constantly pushed and persuaded to leave the moment we're in to pursue new and improved products, personal growth ventures, and other greener grass; where we are told that if we don't embrace change and move forward, we run the risk of not being up to speed and getting left out? I ask my clients to consider that even people who have devoted their entire lives to "living in the moment"—cloistered inhabitants of monasteries and seminaries—work hard to quiet their minds enough to bask in the rapture of time standing still. Isn't it ludicrous to presume, I ask, that if the most spiritually advanced people on earth deem "living in the moment" an ambitious dream, we time-pressed, attention-challenged amateurs can do it? I advise my clients that aspiring to live in the moment will very likely bring them the peace of mind they yearn for, but only if they come up with a "live in the moment" concept that makes sense for the times we live in.

The first step to transforming "living in the moment" from an unreasonable, stress-producing standard to a productive, attainable goal is to take your intellect out of it. Time is not something we can literally grab onto and manipulate, so a deliberate decision to live in the moment by thinking certain thoughts—for instance, "I will be present" or "I am completely immersed where I am right now"—will only magnify the sensation of time moving by. The harder you try to embrace the moment you're in, the more detached from the moment you will be, and the more elusive it will become. The best approach is to simply start by throwing your hands up, giving in to time, and saying to yourself, "I can't stop time and I can't control time and that's okay." Once you give up trying to hold time hostage, once you stop trying to grab onto it, you will actually experience the sensation of time opening up a little bit and giving you more room to move and breathe.

The next step to realistically living in the moment is to approach the task from a sensory rather than an intellectual perspective. Instead of willing yourself to enjoy each moment of your life, which is a ridiculously tall order considering that many moments of life are just plain dull and not worth savoring, strive instead to navigate some moments of your life with your senses whenever you think of it. Make it a habit to stop and notice, at various points throughout your day, what you are seeing, hearing, touching, tasting, and smelling. Take in information through all of your senses. Go beyond the words on your computer screen, the familiar face across the table, or whatever else is right in front of you and drink in the nuances. Feeling the air on your skin, noticing the color of your friend's shirt, taking in the aroma of dinner cooking, discerning one instrument from another in a song on the radio, savoring the flavor of the coffee you're drinking deepens the experience of various moments so that you appreciate them more and remember them better.

Another way to pragmatically live in the moment is to accept that "living in the moment" is not always an agreeable experience. We are led to believe by media messages that living in the moment is all about pushing away off-putting noise and negativity and being one with stabilizing, centering joy and tranquility. While it's certainly true that slowing down and being more present is a way to enjoy the ease of cheer, delight, and other pleasurable emotions, it is more true that uncomfortable feelings like anxiety and grief are apt to arise when you slow down and let emotions float up—especially if slowing down is something new and pent-up emotions are waiting to greet you.

Aspiring to live in the moment means making room in your life for your emotions to be heard and reckoned with, no matter how unappealing, frightening, or inconvenient those emotions may be. The more you organize your life around the emotional experiences that are integral to real adult growth—taking sufficient time away from work either to celebrate the birth of a new family member or to mourn the death of a loved one, for example—the more you will feel that you have really been there for the important events of your life. Meeting your emotions in the present, rather than putting them on hold to be dealt with later or maybe never, frees up the energy and focus needed to be as present as possible amid everyday distractions.

Another aspect to rationally living in the moment is taking control where you can by reducing the interruptions that splinter the moments of your day. Time appears to go by more quickly when it is intruded upon, so you can create the experience of time slowing down and the moment lingering simply by minimizing as best you can the disruptions in your life. Turning your cell phone and Blackberry on only at specific times to check and return messages is one way to do this. Regularly scheduling opportunities for your mind to wander in solitude—walking in nature or driving without the radio—is another way. The more you expose yourself to periods where you don't have to be on the alert for incoming beeps, rings, and other invasive signals for your attention, the more you will experience the moments of your life as expansive and significant.

One more important element of living reasonably in the moment is living within your means. What takes us out of the moment we're in is regret about the past and worry about the future, emotional states we can avoid by managing money prudently and making the most of available resources. Resisting the impulse to acquire more than you need or can afford and taking the time to manage your money prudently will lead you to an increasingly calm and confident state of mind. And spending your money cautiously, buying only what you truly want and desire deep down only when you have the disposable cash, will help you to slow your rate of consumption and ground yourself more fully (and appreciatively) with what you already have.

A final key to living rationally in the moment is taking the concept figuratively. Seeking to live in the moment literally by being present in each and every second only creates an unnecessary sense of urgency. A more do-able goal is to view "the moment" more generally as a stage or chapter of your life. If you succeed at applying the reasonable in-the-moment strategies I've outlined here most of the time—not the impossible all of the time—you will be able to look back at this part of your life knowing that you did the best you could to embrace the overall episode you were in. What the appeal of living in the moment comes down to, after all, is our desire to be able to look back and conclude that we participated as fully as possible in life. What that means in this day and age is reaching the end of your life and saying, "Considering how fast life was moving, and how much pressure there was to do it all, have it all, and be it all, I did a pretty good job of being present for the important things."

Apply the Wisdom

- What was your definition of "living in the moment" before you read this chapter? What is your definition now? How might your current definition reduce the stress in your life?

- Consider ways you might slow down your experience of time to make the moments of your life more enjoyable and memorable. How might you enhance certain parts of your day to make them more pleasurable? Perhaps you could play soothing music while you work on a difficult project. Maybe you could make dinner more interesting by literally adding some spice. Or you might liven up your office or living room by bringing in a bowl of fresh fruit or putting some inspiring artwork on your walls. Think of other ways you can add value to the moments of your life.

- The next time you're sensing time rushing by, try slowing down by living through your senses. Stop thinking and focus on what your eyes are looking at, what your nose is smelling, what your fingers are touching, what your ears are hearing, what your tongue is tasting. How do you feel when you give your brain a break and let your senses take over?

- One reason time seems to go faster and faster the older we get is that much of what we do is routine, and so we move through much of our day without stopping to take note. Try approaching ordinary activities a little differently, more slowly and with curiosity, as if you are going through them for the first time. See if mundane moments become more memorable. Peel, dissemble, and eat a tangerine deliberately, for example, taking note of the textures, tastes, and colors you encounter. Take a shower with the lights off and really feel the sensations of warm water and soap on your body, and become

aware of the contours of your body by touch.   Agree
that you'll whisper to each other at a meal with family
or friends, and see what it's like to *really* pay attention.
Look up at the sky and discern all the different hues
of blue (or gray) you observe. Or listen carefully while
walking a familiar route and make out the many distinct
sounds you detect.

- When you're doing something you really enjoy—eating
  a mouth-watering treat, conversing with a good friend,
  listening to a favorite piece of music—imagine that you
  are engaged in this experience for the last time. See if
  time seems to slow down when you don't take it for
  granted.

- Do you feel that money is a factor in your inability to
  focus on the present? Are you unable to appreciate what
  you have because you are preoccupied with what you
  need to bring in, add on, improve on? Are you unable to
  enjoy your current circumstances because poor financial
  decisions are haunting you? Would better financial
  planning and tighter budgeting help you to get more
  out of what you already have and reduce your financial
  woes?

{ chapter 15 }
Figure Out What You Don't Want

Picture yourself, after months of putting it off, cleaning out a dusty old attic crammed full of junk. You open up boxes and trunks and uncover things you didn't even know existed, and pretty soon the attic is messier than it was when you started. But you keep at it. You're undaunted by the expanding disorder because you know that if you keep throwing away and rearranging, the attic will eventually be organized and dust-free. What you're left with after such careful dismantling, scrutinizing, purging, and rearranging are only the items you absolutely, unequivocally treasure and/or need —along with sufficient space for anything you might want to bring up to the attic in the future. Sweaty, dirty, and tired after such a grueling process, you head down the attic stairs for a reviving, cleansing, and much deserved shower. And as the warm water washes over you, clearing away the sweat and dirt and the weight of all that procrastinating, you feel satisfied, refreshed, and a whole lot lighter.

The point of getting rid of what you don't want—in your attic or in any other area of life, for that matter—is that unburdening yourself of what no longer holds value clears the way for what can bring you greater fulfillment. We lose sight in a culture obsessed with acquiring and possessing that outdated stuff—not just concrete stuff like junk in attics but worn out beliefs, thoughts, and other stuff of the mind; expired relationships, obligations, and commitments in the social world—prevents us from seeing our way clearly to what really will make us happy. In an era where more is always marketed as better, we are too preoccupied with adding on and advancing to realize the mental toll of unremitting acquisition. Many of us believe the prevalent media message that we will achieve greater success, peace of mind, resolution, clarity, enlightenment, or whatever form of composure we're after if we just pile on one more thing, read one more book, attend one more seminar, make one more social networking contact. But much to the dismay of marketers everywhere, the opposite is true. Adding on to our already overstuffed lives will surely only increase the gap between feeling stressed and feeling calm, while putting a temporary freeze on acquisition and whittling down what we already have to what is essential will absolutely make that gap smaller.

Fortunately, narrowing down all the stuff in your life to make more room for what truly is necessary and desirable is a task for which you are already well trained. As we age, most of us experience what I believe to be the very best part of growing older: increasing self-knowledge and associated discernment about what we like and what we don't like, what interests us and what doesn't. Think back to your youth and recall how much lower your standards were, how much more leeway you allowed, how much broader your categories were—quite often to your detriment—simply because you didn't have the life experience to be assertive and discriminating. When you started dating, physical attraction was all it took to create a long-term crush, and you put up with all sorts of personalities and behaviors you'd never tolerate now—all because you didn't know better. If you liked adventure or suspense or romantic entertainment themes, any adventure, suspense, or romantic movie or book would do and you devoured them all. When you got into music, you collected all the albums from pop, rock, new wave, punk, or whatever categories appealed most to you.

As a self-conscious and curious teenager and young adult, you hadn't yet developed the savvy and self-esteem to narrow down your choices according to honed, self-assured knowledge. Now, as an adult, your life is more distinct and straightforward because you base your selections on specific tastes and preferences that you've refined through experimentation and maturity. Physical attraction won't necessarily lead to a date unless your romantic prospect shares your values and treats you with respect. You may still love suspense and adventure, but you'll only see those movies and read those books if they get favorable reviews by the critics you admire. Rock could still be your favorite music, but you only listen to the artists you deem supremely talented.

Nevertheless, though you're pretty set on what makes you tick and what you're into at this stage of life, you are most likely not totally sure of yourself and your choices because you are constantly pressured by society to second-guess your decisions and further expand your horizons. Stopping, sorting, and subtracting seem counter-productive in this do it all, have it all, be it all era. Even the most discerning adults find it difficult to slow down long enough to sort through all they've accumulated and do away with what's no longer working. Though it's hard to go against the grain—as hard as it is to roll up your sleeves and tackle a jumbled attic—a relentless, laser-focused personal inventory is essential for any adult who wants to feel more focused, directed, and resilient in the face of overwhelm.

What it comes down to is this: before you can establish what personal improvements you genuinely want to make, what new products you really need to buy, what services and endeavors you truly want to invest in, what social connections are worth initiating, you have to create room. And making room requires the preliminary messy work of rifling through what you've already accumulated. Taking an honest personal inventory means getting a closer look at every area of your life—home, work, community, finances, relationships, health, and other important categories—and facing unblinkingly what is no longer serving you. You may realize upon ruthless reflection that the once fabulous, expensive living room furniture ensemble is no longer your style, that you don't want to continue with a volunteer commitment, that the magazines you used to look forward to reading every month are now just piling up in a stack on your floor, that you will never again fit into those size six clothes hanging in your closet, that you aren't really into that monthly lunch date with your old college friend anymore, or that you're in a romantic relationship or job more out of comfort than passion. The goal is to decide what is merely taking up space and not contributing to your life in a meaningful way.

Beyond your attachments to pastimes, objects, and people, taking a painstaking personal inventory involves thoroughly assessing your goals, dreams, expectations, and beliefs to determine cognitive contents that may be cluttering your mind. Perhaps goals that were once inspiring to you, such as losing that last ten pounds or getting the corner office, are now tired and stale and just getting in your way. Maybe once motivating expectations of yourself—you should always return email and voicemail within 24 hours or be up on all your professional reading at all times—have become unreasonable in light of your ever-expanding email inbox and ever increasing access to professional updates. Or perhaps long-held convictions about yourself and the world, such as you don't deserve to be successful or that people can't be trusted, just can't be tolerated anymore when you need all the confidence and faith you can muster to effectively evaluate the expansive array of new and improved options before you.

Taking a personal inventory also involves recognizing the seemingly insignificant irritations in your life that, taken together, weigh you down and create stress. You may think the dry-cleaning you haven't picked up, a library book you haven't returned, your unwashed car, a thank-you note you've been meaning to write are just trivial tasks that don't matter much in the scheme of things. But all those minor items on your to-do list add up and wear you down by subtly nagging for your attention. Even if they're so far at the back of your mind that you don't even think about them, those chores you deem inconsequential are taking up room and preventing clear thinking.

The hard part of figuring out what you don't want is dealing with the emotions that can arise when you come to terms with what's no longer your cup of tea. An emphasis on what's not working can lead to anger at yourself for being impulsive and making mistakes in the past. Realizing you've outgrown your career, social circle, significant other, geographic location, or any other substantial part of your life can be terrifying as you contemplate the major risks and transitions you will have to endure to set things right. The important thing to keep in mind as you decide what to keep and what to leave behind is that past decisions, no matter how misguided they may seem in retrospect, have helped shape your capacity to know what is right for you now. There's no need to make big changes until you feel ready. Just clarifying what you don't want—even if you don't yet have the guts or a plan to get rid of it—will give you the mental energy and space required to start clearing the way. Take your time and start with the small things. Slowly but surely you will become more certain about what you want to bring into your life and how to make it happen.

Apply the Wisdom

- Sit down with a pad of paper and a pen, and set a timer for 20 minutes. Write down every little errand and annoyance you can think of that's currently weighing on you. This includes fixing that leaky bathroom faucet, returning the hedge clippers you borrowed from your neighbor last summer, canceling that credit card you never use, taking your car in for an oil change. Once you've finished the list, resolve to tackle each item one by one. See how you feel as you cross each pesky chore off.

- Reserve a weekend for getting rid of clutter. Clothes you haven't worn in a year, once cherished keepsakes that don't mean much to you now, books and magazines you're never going to find time to read. Notice whether the space you've created inspires ideas for more fitting possessions, along with opportunities to obtain them.

- Make a list of what you know you don't want. Now, ask yourself as you review each item: What's positive about this realization? What have I learned from this? How will this experience get me closer to what I do want? For example, if you've realized that moving to a big city was a mistake, you might feel grateful that you no longer have to fantasize about the glamour of urban life and you may have a much better idea about where you want to settle. If you've realized that you're not happy in your romantic relationship, you might recognize the communication skills you're gained from dealing with a difficult person and you may have a better idea of what you're looking for in your next relationship. You'll see that your mistakes have not been all for naught; you've gained a greater sense of who you are—and what you want —from all of them.

- Complete these sentences quickly, going with your first impulse:

I am _____.

The world is _____.

My parents are _____.

Men are _____.

Women are _____.

People are _____.

I can't _____.

I must _____.

I can _____.

Now consider which of these statements serve you and which don't. What new beliefs might serve you better? Personal convictions are stubborn because they probably made sense at one time of your life—like maybe it was wise to believe you had to be hyperalert as a child if you were raised by irresponsible parents, but now you are an adult in charge of yourself and it's probably okay to be less vigilant. You might want to consider counseling, a support group, or maybe an appropriate course or book to get you started on revising the beliefs that are getting in your way.

- Think back and make lists of your top five goals ten years ago and five years ago. Now make a list of your current top five goals. Notice what goals have changed over the years and what goals, if any, have remained the same. What conclusions can you draw by comparing lists? Maybe you can track your progress by seeing the evolution of your goals. Or maybe you can see that you've been carrying some goals with you too long. Circle the goals from your current list that resonate with you and cross off the ones that don't. Consider letting go of goals that seem like a burden—or rephrase them to make them more motivating. For example, if your goal to exercise more frequently has become old and tired but you still want to lose weight, try making your goal more enticing by reframing it as "have more fun being physically active."

- If you find after taking a thorough personal inventory that your job, primary relationship, house, or any other significant part of your life is no longer working, take a deep breath and remind yourself that there is never a need—unless you are in a toxic, abusive or otherwise dangerous situation—to move quickly. Now determine three small steps you can take—confiding in a close friend, consulting a psychotherapist, taking time out to soul search, writing in your journal, for example —to begin to explore the possibility of change.

{ chapter 16 }
Figure Out What You Do Want

You wouldn't guess this if you met him today at the nursing home where he is bedridden without his faculties in the final stages of Parkinson's Disease, but my father, more than anyone else I've ever encountered, taught me how to make the most of life. Until his devastating illness arrived out of nowhere and took hold of his mind and body about ten years ago, he would wake up most mornings feeling lucky to be alive, viewing the day in front of him as a precious opportunity to learn and grow, contribute to the world, and enjoy himself and those he loves. He filled his time with favorite books, food, music, and people. Endlessly curious, he was always looking into new travel destinations, reading up on fresh topics, asking provocative questions, and experimenting with innovative ideas. Truly appreciative of nature, he loved to walk in the woods, swim in fresh water, and drink in every color of a sunset and every sound of solitude (one of his favorite sounds is the haunting cry of loons on a lake).

Always optimistic, my dad could find humor and possibility in almost any situation. When a problem arose, he'd relish in the challenge of finding a solution. If outdoor plans got snowed or rained out, he'd happily switch gears to an equally satisfying activity: reading or conversing in front of a crackling fire in the fireplace or taking a deep nap to the patter of rain on the roof. He applied himself fully to meaningful work until he retired, and still, after almost 50 years of marriage, he behaves with my mother as if they are on their honeymoon. When I asked him recently, during one of his rare moments of lucidity, if he has any regrets about mistakes made or roads not taken, he responded without hesitation, with complete and utter confidence, "No."

Noticing from an early age my dad's extraordinary knack for living well, and sharing his temperament and ambition, I looked to him as a mentor who could guide me toward increasing fulfillment. As a young girl, that meant taking his cue on what to order at the ice cream parlor, what shows to watch on TV, how to approach a homework assignment, how to make the most of free time on a Sunday afternoon. I would ask him what to do and he would make great suggestions—try the chocolate milkshake, watch *Columbo* with me, break your homework down into small pieces, how about a swim or a hike?—and almost all of his suggestions have led to pastimes and penchants that are still with me today.

But things got tricky with my father when bigger life questions arose in adolescence, such as where should I apply for college and what vocation should I prepare for? Suddenly, because my father's life choices had been more limited when he was my age, his answers—"Just choose a college you like" and "Do whatever you want to do for a living"—seemed overly simplistic and impractical. My father had decided in high school to become a Boys Club of America Executive Director because he'd joined his community Boys Club as a boy and had already worked his way up to camp counselor, swim instructor, and camp waterfront director. He loved the organization and the work, and it just made sense to continue on that track. He chose Boston University for his social work degree because it was a good school and close to home. Another simple decision. So why, my father asked as he looked back on the seamless, obvious professional path he had carved out for himself at my age, did this have to be so difficult for me?

My father couldn't understand where I was coming from because he had decided on a career and college during a time when there weren't so many alternatives. He could see the steady stream of college brochures arriving after the release of my SAT scores, and he knew that career possibilities had more than multiplied since his adolescence, but he didn't seem to get that I was overwhelmed with—rather than liberated by—the choices before me. Plus, because he had launched his career trajectory in childhood, he couldn't relate to a daughter who only knew from all the part-time high school jobs she'd endured, some at his suggestion—day camp counselor, swim instructor, fast food cashier, retail clerk—what she *didn't* want to do.

It was becoming increasingly evident to both of us as I neared high school graduation that, despite our mutual personality traits, hobbies, and respect, there were some very clear and real variances between us that were making it impossible for my father to help me at this stage of my life. Not only could he not relate to my experience of having too many choices, but a difference in interests and values was creating distance. My father, for example, one of those rare people who discover their life calling in youth, knew at my age that he loved working with kids, wanted to get married and start a family soon after college, and wanted to live in a small city. What I was most firm on then was that I didn't want to work with or have my own children, I wanted to marry in my thirties so I could build a career first, and I wanted to live in an exciting big city. After several frustrating attempts to find direction and solace from my father, I realized that it was up to me to figure out what I wanted to do after high school. And so my journey began.

Now, almost 30 years later, as I contemplate the trials and errors and twists and turns of navigating professional and personal decisions many times over, I can say that I have a pretty good handle on how to get to the root of what I really want. Figuring out what you want to do, be, and have can be a complex endeavor in a world where new options are always emerging, but it doesn't have to be crazy-making. The following guidelines should help make the process easier.

Get interfering voices out of the way. Figuring out what you want requires that you determine how much of what you want is influenced by media, family, friends, colleagues, and other sources of direction that you may have internalized as your own intuition. You might think you really want that piece of clothing on sale until you stop and realize that you feel pressured by the voice of your frugal mother warning you never to pass up a good bargain. Just before you say yes to that so-so job you've been offered, you might consider that you're being pushed to settle by the voice of that popular kid in high school who treated you like you weren't good enough to be accepted. Before you follow through on the impulse to eat, sign up for, accept, agree to, or buy something, entertain the probable possibility that you have been led more by advertising than by your gut to take that next step. To ensure you are going after what you want and not what others want you to want, it's wise to question yourself carefully before you act.

Start with the feeling you want. No matter who you are or what you desire, one thing you have in common with every other relatively well-adjusted adult is that you simply want, bottom line, to be happy. Whatever it is you're striving for—from a decent hair cut to a significant other, from a glass of ice water to an oceanfront home, from piano lessons to a masters' degree, from lunch money to a million-dollar stock portfolio—you want what you want because it will make you feel better than you feel right now. So even if you haven't a clue what you want in any area of your life, knowing that you want to feel good is an excellent place to begin.

Let's say you're definitely bored with your house, your job, your car, your vacation routine, your wardrobe, a particular hobby, the contents of your pantry, any area of life or work that has grown tiresome. You are clear on what you want to get rid of but you aren't clear at all on a replacement. You can at least initiate greater clarity by asserting that you want a new house, job, car, vacation destination, whatever it is that will bring you more enjoyment than what you just unloaded. By framing the ensuing exploration stage as an opportunity to find interests, objects, challenges, and interactions that add to your happiness, you will establish a clear-cut litmus test for winnowing down possibilities. If a nursing career, a house in the country, a low-fat diet, or a hybrid car feel good to you at first glance, take your exploration further. Drop what doesn't feel preliminarily good and move on. The advantage of recognizing feeling good as the point of all your goals is that you are always steered positively toward what will enhance your life—and, as you recall from earlier in this book, an optimistic perspective encourages resonant opportunities.

Make the sky your limit. One problem many of us encounter in our efforts to establish what we really want is that we discount options too quickly for reasons that don't necessarily hold up. You may really, truly want a sailboat, but you assume you'll never be able to make enough money to buy one. You may be sure you want to join a choir, but you're convinced you're too old to develop your singing talent. Or you could be positive you want a certain job, but you knock yourself out of the running by telling yourself you'll never be able to beat the competition. It's true that some of your dreams and goals probably are way out of reach—wanting to be an astronaut if you're afraid of heights or play for the NFL if you're over 40 with no football experience. It's also true that some of the goals you deem too lofty may actually be workable. That's why it's important to ignore that critic inside of you and go a little crazy by considering every single goal and dream that crosses your mind. Brainstorming works because it allows you to get your ideas out of your head, see them from a fresh, clear perspective, and find inspiration, ideas, and connections that you didn't know existed.

Make sure you really want what you want. Another obstacle we face as we attempt to clarify what we want is that we don't look deep enough at what we want to ensure we really want it. A job opportunity may seem very attractive because it pays a six-figure salary and it would be wonderful to make so much money. But if you look beneath the surface, you might see that the job requires a lot of what you don't want: long hours and too much time away from family. An invitation to join a prestigious board of directors may sound intriguing because you want to bolster your resume' and expand your business connections. But once you get past feeling flattered, you may admit to yourself that a big part of being on this board is fund-raising, something you absolutely don't want to do. Slowing down to investigate the truth behind what you think you want is difficult in a culture that urges us to make decisions quickly so that we can move on to the next choice, but taking the time to see the full picture beyond your first reaction will help you avoid mistakes.

Let your values and objectives guide you. Clients often ask me for input on serious matters: Should they leave a partner who has cheated and pursue potentially better romantic horizons, or should they continue to work for a jerk or search for a new and hopefully better job? Sometimes they simply ask me to tell them what I'd do in their situation; other times they want me to recommend a particular book or refer them to another professional who may have the answers they seek. I tell these clients that expert advice can be useful only if they consider it against the backdrop of their own personal beliefs and circumstances. Who's to say whether a cheating partner should be left? A young adult might choose to stay with a cheating partner when she realizes that her partner is naive and confused and has potential for growth, whereas a long-married man may decide to leave after accepting that his wife is not going to change. Similarly, a young man in his first job may decide that working for a jerk is worth it because he's getting great experience, while a more experienced colleague may decide enough is enough because he's way past earning his stripes. Qualified experts can offer you sound advice, but you have to assess that advice to ensure it fits your current priorities and ideas.

Be honest about your intentions. It's hard sometimes to get to the bottom of what we want because our motives can be complex. To avoid working hard to acquire something you thought you wanted but really don't want in the end, it's important to be real with yourself about your expectations. Before you buy that expensive car, be sure you want it because you will adore driving it and not because you want to impress your boss with the showy brand. If you're seriously thinking about a major life-changing step like cosmetic surgery, understand that you'll still have the same issues to wrestle with in your tuned-up body. We Americans are addicted to the thrill of buying shiny, new things because we feel instantly better—but that instant feeling is usually temporary. If you find yourself wanting something because you hope it will fill a hole inside you, know that the only way to feel better is to do the hard work of learning to love yourself.

Know how much you want to put yourself out there. There is no shortage of ideas out there for getting what you want from life and work—the faster the better. If you're tired of being part of the rat race, you can start your own business. If you want to take a luxurious vacation, you can put it on your credit card. If you want to increase your confidence, you can enroll in any number of empowering personal growth adventures. Whether or not these ideas sound good to you, however, depends on how much risk you want to assume. Just because money is available to borrow doesn't mean you feel comfortable taking on debt. Self-employment may be a viable way to work according to your own agenda, but it's not reasonable at all if you don't want to deal with the uncertainty of launching and sustaining your own enterprise. Challenging personal development programs can take you to enthralling new levels of fulfillment, but only if you want to challenge your existing style of functioning. As you contemplate what you want, it's important to consider how far you are willing to go outside your comfort zone to make it happen.

Consider better alternative ways to getting what you want. Sometimes we are so intent on getting whatever it is we want that we become closed to more reasonable ways of getting it. Let's say you want to be more creative and you're convinced that the only way to accomplish that goal is to leave your job in banking and get a job in advertising. Maybe there's an easier way to be more creative, like keeping your banking job and taking some art classes or joining an acting group. Perhaps you want to improve your marriage, and you're convinced that the only solution is to enroll with your spouse in an intensive (and expensive) couples therapy retreat. Maybe just talking with your spouse will open up some easier, more affordable ways to fortify your relationship. Or maybe you've always craved the excitement and camaraderie of playing on a professional sports team and you haven't considered that a community team would feel just as good at this time of your life. If you want something that feels out of reach, you can make it more feasible by opening your mind to other scenarios that could bring you similar fulfillment.

Test drive what you want. Oftentimes people will come to me feeling frantic because they've just starting dating someone and they're not sure if the relationship is going to work out, or they've just interviewed for a job that they're not convinced they want. It's important to remember in these situations that we can take time to make a decision, and, in fact, that's the whole purpose of dating and interviewing. If you're thinking about buying a summer home, rent a few different homes nearby for short vacations to get a better feel for the area before you commit. Likewise, bring fabric and paint swatches home and sit with them a while before you make final interior decorating decisions. Take a few courses part time to make sure you like the new field you're considering before you quit your job and go back to school full time. No important decision should be made before you know what you're working with, so it's best to experiment and sample until you have enough information to warrant a final choice.

Know when to sacrifice for the sake of getting what you want. Sometimes what you want may conflict with other things you want, and you may have to let go and forfeit those other things to reach a more important goal. If you want to make more money in your field, for example, you may have to live on less money for a while in order to invest in a higher degree. If you want to improve your health, you may have to cut back on some of the fattening foods you love and use your treasured leisure time for exercising. If you want to be more discerning with your social life, you may have to get used to being alone more often. The payoff for these kinds of trade-offs, of course, is that you ultimately achieve your greater want and end up happier.

Apply the Wisdom

- The next time you feel the impulse to do something—
  like accept a lunch invitation or buy a certain product—
  take a step back and give yourself room to really think
  about what you're doing. Do you really want to accept
  that lunch invitation or are you just feeling obligated?
  Do you really want that new product or has advertising
  convinced you that you should want it? Try this exercise
  a few more times to see if you get better at distinguishing
  between your own inner voice and outside influences.

- Get a large sheet of paper and write in large letters in
  the middle: *what feels good*. Now write down everything
  you can possibly think of that fits that category. Step
  back and critique what you've come up with by asking:
  Will this really help me feel good, or is there something
  I'm missing? If you've written "BMW convertible," for
  example, you may decide upon closer consideration that
  making car payments for such an expensive vehicle and
  worrying about theft and damage may not feel so good
  after all.

- Think about something you want to bring into your
  life. Maybe you want a new job, a better relationship, a
  nicer yard, or improved health. Get out a sheet of paper,
  write what you want at the top of the page, and then
  draw a big circle underneath. All around the outside
  of the circle list all the qualities you don't desire in a
  situation. For example, if a new house is what you want,
  write all the features you don't want that house to have,
  like unaffordable mortgage payments, noisy neighbors,
  insufficient light. Inside the circle list all the qualities you
  desire in the situation or object you want. For example,
  if a new job is what you want, write down all the
  features you want that new job to have, such as room for
  advancement, collegial environment, great benefits, easy
  commute. If you're not sure on the details of whatever it

is that you want, just write down how you will feel when you get what you want. For example, if you want a better relationship but you don't have a particular partner in mind, you may already know that you want to feel respected in the relationship, that you want your next partner to share your sense of humor, and that you want to feel loved and be loved. After you've completed your circle, see if you are clearer about what you want. Add to your circle as more ideas come to you.

- Make a list of all the things you can think of that you've ever talked yourself out of wanting because it seemed implausible at the time. Go over each item and ask: Do I still want this, and, if so, is there a way to make it possible? Consider asking a few positive, supportive people in your life if they can see ways to bring some of these goals to fruition.

- Take a long walk by yourself someplace quiet. Notice the true wants and needs that surface inside you when you're away from the clatter of your everyday routine.

- Make a list of any self-defeating personal beliefs that might be getting in the way of figuring out what you really want. Do you believe you don't deserve to be happy? Do you believe you must depend on others to steer your life in the right direction? Do you believe it's selfish to take time to get in touch with what you want? Do you believe you don't have the ability to accomplish your goals, so why bother? If you find that your negative beliefs are so entrenched that you can't overcome them on your own, consider engaging the support of an experienced therapist.

{ chapter 17 }
Enlist the Internet in Getting What You Want

When 17-year-old Kay Wheeler decided to launch the first Elvis Presley Fan Club in 1956, one of her biggest challenges was finding a suitable photograph of The King that she could copy and distribute to fans. Can you imagine in this age of information overwhelm that such a quandary ever existed? Fortunately Kay was uncommonly brazen and tenacious back in the day when celebrity photos were actually hard to track down. We've come a long way since news came in sanitized one-size-fits-all increments, suitable for all ages and all watercooler conversations, and celebrity gossip was glossed over by agents and other handlers before it got to the press. But there really was a time when if you wanted information beyond what was available in the daily newspaper, in monthly magazines, or on a smattering of TV and radio shows you had to possess either superb connections, superior sleuthing skills, or both.

Now, thanks to incredible advancements in technology since Kay started her fan club, a similar feat could be accomplished with just a few clicks on a computer keyboard. It's possible to find photographs of almost anyone—famous or not—just by doing a routine Google search. Information is so widely available today in so many forms and at so many levels that the challenge has evolved from finding certain data to sorting through it and narrowing it all down. Of course, that's why so many adults feel so daunted. We realize that the information we had access to before the internet was just the tip of the iceberg. There is so much more beneath the surface, and the sheer breadth and depth can be exhausting to contemplate.

The internet is still a fairly new cultural phenomenon, so many of us who were well into our adult years when we sent our first email and did our first online search are still trying to figure out how to assimilate the internet into everyday life. Because change requires the hard work of re-training our brains to do things differently, it's easier sometimes to rationalize that we can get along just fine without adapting. For some of us who would rather flat out reject the internet than take the time and energy to see how it actually might be a good thing for us, we invent stories to make our resistance seem like a wise choice. We tell ourselves that the internet is destructive because it discourages real live contact between people; it exposes children to predators, violence, sex, and other evils; it is a bottomless, addictive well of darkness that sucks users away from fresh air and activity and into obesity and isolation. More open-minded adults recognize the value of the internet but, intimidated by the sheer enormity of it, use it only peripherally. Adults of this category typically send emails regularly, use Facebook and other popular social networking sites, and surf the web occasionally when they have a specific need or a little down time, but they shy away from accessing the internet more intimately for fear that learning its ins and outs will take too much time and they might get pulled away from important responsibilities.

The truth of the matter is that the internet, just like TV, fattening foods, and alcohol, can absolutely be a dangerous distraction if used in extreme ways without moderation. But if you approach the internet with a spirited sense of adventure and purpose, you can experience all the advantages it has to offer. Getting to know the internet does take time and effort, but the payoff is that life becomes immensely easier. In other words, it is possible to make the internet a vital part of your routine—without losing control of yourself and ending up fixated, fat, and friendless.

In my own efforts to integrate the internet into my life, I have observed people, mostly adolescents and young adults and some computer literate adults, who are not only completely undaunted by the internet but also view the internet as an indispensable asset. It's easy to say that young people embrace the internet so readily because they have grown up with it and that technologically advanced adults are comfortable with it because they have the right skills to navigate it. But that's just part of the story. I am convinced that only one simple piece of knowledge separates internet enthusiasts from tentative users. Young or old, technical or not, those who are most at ease with the internet know what the rest of us don't: *you can take what you want from the internet and leave the rest.*

Just because the internet offers us infinite access to information doesn't mean that we have to use all or any of it. The internet is a world unto itself and, like the real world, it contains sufficient variety to appeal to everyone in some way. Some people fear this appeal. They're afraid that once they really get into the internet, they will never be able to drag themselves away because so much will pique their interest and test their resolve. Actually most of what's on the internet is completely irrelevant to you or just plain junk. By exploring the internet with a plan of action, you can bypass the extraneous, find the particular sites and services that will meet your specific requirements, and feel much more knowledgeable and in command.

The key to getting from the internet what suits you best is to approach it as you would a city you're visiting for the first time on vacation. Knowing that you can't possibly work in every sight there is to see, you come up with a list of diversions that most grab you and plan a reasonable itinerary. If you want to experience an idyllic weekend in the Big Apple, for example, you don't just fly into LaGuardia and wander around aimlessly with no idea of what you're going to do next; you arrive with a hotel reservation and some ideas of neighborhoods you want to explore, museums you want to check out, shows you want to see, and restaurants you want to try. Similarly, using the internet productively involves knowing what you want and need *before you log on* so that you can access the internet in line with your specific goals and desires.

The first step to making the internet work for you is to determine why you *don't* need or want it. Mainstream information sources are still perfectly viable, so if you like to keep current with the local TV news, there's no reason to do anything differently. If you want your news delivered from a particular slant, however, there are plenty of alternative online newspapers available to suit your specific perspective. You can search your options and take your pick. Likewise, if you enjoy dinner and a movie out every now and then but don't consider yourself a food connoisseur or movie buff, it's just fine to peruse movie listings and restaurant reviews in the local paper or get recommendations from friends. But if you're looking for the most exquisite plate of pasta primavera within a 100-mile radius or want to read what your top three movie critics have to say about a certain film before you'll commit, there are countless internet sites that can help you make the right selections.

The beauty of the internet is that it can be a doorway to your passions—at any time of day or night, from any location. Whatever you are into, no matter how obscure your pastime, you can go deeper with your interest and connect with other enthusiasts almost effortlessly. Sheila, who lives in Florida and longs to live in France, practices her French by regularly reading three favorite French blogs and tuning into French radio stations. Ken, a bonds trader, unwinds from his stressful job at night by delving into his heritage via several genealogy websites. Sandy, a trained opera singer, gave up singing as a career to go into business but stays connected with her former peers by logging onto opera chat rooms. The internet can't replicate the aroma of fresh French pastries baking, the camaraderie of performing in a singing troupe, or talking in person with those who share your unique fascination, but Sheila, Ken, and Sandy all agree that it enriches their lives by keeping them involved with their distinct hobbies at an intensity that simply wouldn't be possible without technology.

Many enlightened adults appreciate the internet for the sake of convenience. If you know what you want, there is no better way to find what you're looking for—quite often at a discount. Maria loves shopping for clothes and home goods but has three children to care for, so she doesn't get out much. Her solution is to shop online when the kids are sleeping. Erin, the consummate coupon clipper, uses the internet to find the best deals on food before she heads to the grocery store. And Rick, a newly divorced father of two, finds easy, kid-friendly recipes through a few favorite websites devoted to busy single parents.

One of the biggest internet benefits is its entertainment value. Whereas stores can carry only a certain number of books or DVDs due to limited shelf space, shelfless online emporiums like Amazon and Netflix can offer infinite titles ranging from unheard of to blockbuster. And endless diversion is available through YouTube and myriad game sites. Leanne, an insurance saleswoman, lifts her spirits up after difficult sales calls by watching funny YouTube videos. Joan, who recently moved from California to Texas, keeps in touch with a former colleague by playing Scrabble with him online. Shawn, an accountant, eases the monotony of exercising by downloading nightly talk shows and watching them on his laptop while running on his treadmill.

The internet also simplifies the world of work in innumerable ways. Adults who once felt isolated when working from home now feel much more connected thanks to professional networking sites and online forums. Journalists, attorneys, and other professionals whose jobs require research are now able to cut down considerably on travel time by being able to access the information they need from their computers. People of every occupation are able to keep up with the latest discoveries in their fields through infinite professional websites and online articles and journals. Specialists of all kinds can easily put their heads together via the internet to solve problems, accelerate inventions and cures, and forge movements. And many adults have become more professionally fulfilled by enrolling in online courses and downloading programs that allow them to learn every kind of trade or skill imaginable.

One more benefit of the internet is smoother and more consistent communication. Julie, who lives far from relatives, has created a website with her family so that everyone can keep in closer touch by posting news and photos in a central place. Denise loves being able to use email for quick contact with clients and relatives who can be overly long-winded over the phone. Cary says he owes his great rapport with his adolescent kids to knowing them more fully through exchanges on Facebook and by reading and commenting on their blogs. Depending entirely on technology to keep in touch can compromise the quality of relationships, but as Julie, Denise, and Cary will tell you, using technology as a complement to face-to-face conversation is an excellent way to strengthen relationships.

The reality is that the internet world is so all-encompassing it can contribute in amazing ways to every single area of your life. Whatever you want—the right primary care physician, a quote for a speech you're preparing, a recipe that calls for the three odd ingredients you happen to have in your fridge, a blog that will keep you up on politics, a background check on a blind date, tips for dealing with a difficult client, access to people who share your love of scuba diving, a list of the best books on increasing your confidence, the cheapest rental car available in Atlanta, the list goes on and on and on—you can find it online. If you make it your goal to use it in ways that enrich rather than engulf you, you will see that the internet can be your personal secretary, your research assistant, your court jester, your travel agent, a virtual superstore at your fingertips. Sure, the internet can be a draining, mind-numbing obsession that pulls you away from reality and takes the substance out of living if you let it. But if you customize the internet to meet your individual needs, it can be your ticket to more seamlessly creating a life you can truly call your own.

Apply the Wisdom

- Consider any interests you have that don't require the internet. Are your current needs and wants being met by the daily newspaper, basic TV, and cookbooks you already own? Would you rather read magazines and books the old-fashioned way than on a computer screen? Do you feel better knowing that you don't need to consult the internet about absolutely everything?

- Based on what you've discovered from reading the last two chapters and this one, make a list of the top five things you want in your life. Your list can include material things like a new job, a renovated living room, an improved wardrobe, and so on. Your list can also include the more abstract, like a better relationship with your spouse, more opportunities to express yourself creatively, advanced emotional intelligence. Once you've made your list, spend about an hour researching the internet for websites, blogs, and other online ways to expand your awareness in your top five areas of interest.

- Consider ways you might use the internet more astutely for the sake of convenience. Research sites that can get you deals and discounts, help you with travel arrangements, and make shopping for clothes, household goods, and other staples more manageable.

- Think about ways you use the internet for entertainment. How might you use it more productively to amuse yourself, reduce stress, have fun, and unwind? Surf the web with the intent of finding some new games to try, watch a few YouTube videos, download some podcasts by your favorite comedians. Now think about ways you can use internet amusement to break up your day and bring laughter into your life.

- One reason adults feel so overwhelmed by the internet is that emails and favorite websites build up. Take some time to do an internet clean sweep, deleting emails and favorite websites that are no longer valuable or pertinent. As is always the way with clutter, getting rid of what you don't want anymore will make room for new and better opportunities.

- Try making the internet more manageable by distinguishing between work-related and personal internet use. This means perhaps spending an hour or so working on a professional project and then taking some time to update your Facebook page, post your old bike on Craigslist, and order flowers for a friend rather than switching over and over between business and pleasure. You'll find that more gets done – and you have more fun – when you don't waste time and energy going back and forth.

- Use the internet more mindfully, and not just on impulse, by turning your computer on at designated times and keeping it off when you don't want to be tempted. You're much less likely to get pulled into mindless internet surfing when cyberspace is more than a click away.

- If you feel really overwhelmed by the internet, consider asking a tech-savvy friend or professional to show you how to employ the internet more efficiently. The right consultant can help you to customize your internet use to your specific needs and desires.

{ chapter 18 }
Set Reasonable Goals

Rome wasn't built in a day. The Mayflower didn't arrive at Plymouth Rock overnight. And America's independence from Britain didn't happen on one hot summer afternoon in 1776. Perhaps because we learn about historical triumphs from distilled, abbreviated versions of the long, drawn-out truth, we expect to achieve our personal goals in full, flawless sweeps. For the sake of fitting our heritage neatly into textbooks and television shows, the false starts and frustrations involved in any kind of major feat are whittled down into deceptively tidy inspirational legends. As we strive to fulfill our individual longings, what we get when we look to our shared past for incentive is the misleading message that we should be able to accomplish our aspirations smoothly and speedily—without second-guessing or stalling.

Most of us living in the modern age are by our very nature ambitious go-getters with a healthy drive to better ourselves and our world by setting and reaching lofty goals. We hail, after all, from ancestors whose desire for greater liberty and opportunity led to the founding of countries, the collapse of stifling regimes, and countless time-saving inventions— from the automobile to the fax machine—that free us up for realizing the very dreams that beckon us. But experienced as we are at recognizing our desire and need to improve our lives and devoted as we are to enriching our circumstances, we fall utterly short when it comes to conceiving reasonable strategies for making those changes happen.

In our fast-paced culture, we conjure up perfectly legitimate dreams with the comparatively crazy expectation that we must realize our visions instantly. Somehow we believe that putting this kind of pressure on ourselves to perform will propel us forward. What happens, of course, is that we sabotage our success with goals so daunting that they trigger a fear and flight reaction. *No way can I switch careers/paint my house/write a book/lose 50 pounds just like that!* We stop in our tracks before we even begin. Our aspirations are motivating, but our unreasonable approach—go from A to Z this minute!—is paralyzing. So we go back and forth, back and forth between wanting something to happen and realizing we just don't have what it takes to make it happen now. Each swing of this pendulum seems to confirm that we must lack the guts, the brains, the willpower, the luck, or some ever elusive goal-manifesting power, when the only thing we're really missing is a sensible game plan.

Whatever you've decided you want to bring into your life by the time you read this chapter, there's only one way to attract those things successfully, and that's *one step at a time.* I know you want to make dramatic strides and I wish I could help you, but breaking your goals down into manageable phases is the only way that really works.

Think about it for a minute.

All the skills and smarts you acquired as a child, before you started demanding on-the-spot results from yourself, came gradually. Very gradually. You learned everything from walking and talking to setting the table and riding your bike through a series of very small shifts and stages. You moved from writing your name to writing term papers, adding two plus two to figuring geometric theorems over the course of several grades, umpteen instructions, and a multitude of homework assignments. You've advanced through academic and social lessons because the lessons were structured— challenging enough to be stimulating but not so challenging that you froze in fear at the very thought of advancing toward them.

Children have no issue with taking small steps because they haven't yet bought into the cockeyed logic of adult achievement that says small goals aren't worth the effort because they won't really get you anywhere. We adults have lost touch with what most children know: that we get the most done when we feel creative and confident, not when we feel overwhelmed and intimidated.

One beauty of a small goal is simply that it let's you *get started*—and getting started is crucial because that's when the magic happens. Every masterpiece begins with a single musical note, brush stroke, or written word. It is the act of crossing that line between apprehension and creation that liberates your mind, frees your ideas, and lets your intuition take the lead. Once that first step is in motion, the goal begins to manifest. Because the secret to starting is outwitting your fear, taking a stride so small that your inner critic sleeps right through it is the way to proceed. All you have to do to get going is decide on a series of steps so ridiculously, laughably, insanely doable that self-doubt doesn't stand a chance of getting in your way.

If you're like most time-pressed Americans, you may think, "If I take small steps, it'll take way too long to reach my goals." I understand where you're coming from, but I want to assure you that, contrary to this false logic, taking small steps actually helps you achieve your goals more quickly than you ever thought possible.

Here's why.

With the satisfaction that comes from completing that first small step, you will feel more confident, motivated, and ready for step two, step three, and so on. Whereas big goals sap your strength and stamina by triggering draining emotions like anxiety and self-doubt, small goals encourage the positive emotions and energy that invigorate real growth and accomplishment. The goal of cleaning your house may actually exhaust you more than the cleaning itself. However, that first small step of picking up three pairs of socks from your bedroom floor may be surprisingly inspiring. The big goal of finding a new job may send you into a panic, but a first step of placing a bouquet of flowers on your desk may nudge you toward feeling more worthy of a better career opportunity.

Something to keep in mind as you consider various goals you might want to take a crack at reasonably is that a primary reason people have trouble accomplishing their goals is that they don't have what they need—the necessary supplies or space or frame of mind—for the job. If your goal is to write an article, you'll need a computer and a comfortable, inspiring workplace free of distractions. If you want to learn to salsa dance, you'll require appropriate shoes and clothing. If you want a raise at work, you'll need to research your rationale before meeting with your boss. You will be more apt to succeed at whatever you set your mind to if you incorporate any important prep work into your small steps.

One more important thing to consider about goal setting is that goals are accomplished more quickly when you reward yourself along the way. When you don't reward yourself—either because you consider rewards kid stuff or not worth the money or because you don't think you deserve or need compensation for your work—you risk losing momentum at best and sabotaging your success at worst. The really cool thing here is that compensation doesn't have to be complicated to provide powerful incentive. Rewards can be anything meaningful to you—a new CD, lunch with a friend, a favorite magazine, a stroll through your favorite neighborhood, a nap—that adequately expresses appreciation to yourself for a job well done.

To stay motivated and charged as you move forward, encourage yourself with small but appealing incentives bit by bit, much like you'd reward a dog biscuits at every point of learning a new trick. Then, when you've reached your final goal, you can reward yourself more handsomely—perhaps taking a vacation when you've arrived at your ideal weight, arranging a spa day for yourself after you've organized your house, subscribing to a season at the local theater when you've overcome your TV addiction.

One final point: goals get accomplished when they feel good. Some goals are easier to feel good about than others. A goal to decorate your house may feel good if you enjoy shopping for lamps and rugs and are comfortable picking paint colors. And a goal to get in shape may feel good if you love being active and already know how to exercise and eat well. But if you don't feel excited about or up for working on something—even if you really, really want it—you'll have trouble being successful. If you're invested in accomplishing a particular goal but find that the process is burdening you, try rewarding yourself more frequently. Ten minutes of your favorite internet activity after every ten minutes of filing papers. Listening to books on tape or music as you clean in half-hour increments. Exercising with a friend. Writing down five reasons why you deserve a new job every time you sit down to work on your resumé. By creating a manageable strategy and compensating yourself sufficiently, you can create the incentive to get almost anything done.

Apply the Wisdom

- List three small things you can do to feel better about your bedroom. Maybe a change of sheets, a scented candle on your bedside table, or a few new hangers would help. You decide. Just make sure the steps feel easy.

- List three small things you can do to feel better about your workspace. You might clear off your desk, dump your wastebasket, or put an inspiring quote on your bulletin board. Remember to make sure your steps feel easy!

- Choose a life area you want to improve. It could be your home environment, your career, your physical health, your relationship with yourself, any area you think it would feel good to work on. Now list three small steps you can take toward feeling just a little bit better in that area.

- Make a list of small rewards that would motivate you to get started on one of the above plans of action. And make sure your reward is really a reward, not something you'd give yourself regardless. For example, if you always get coffee in the afternoon, then coffee isn't sufficient. Make it a specialty coffee drink, or, better yet, reward yourself with a new coffee mug.

- Test at least one plan of action above and reward yourself accordingly.

{ chapter 19 }
Nurture Your Progress

Samantha, a jewelry designer, had been working steadily for several months on a collection to unveil at the most popular crafts show in her state. She lost momentum two weeks before the show, missed her deadline, and canceled at the last minute, forfeiting her deposit and losing out on her most important promotion opportunity of the year. Brian, a project manager for a telecommunications company, excels at leading large teams through the complicated process of conceptualizing and carrying out multifaceted ventures. He recently applied his strategic expertise to developing a well paced plan to train for his first marathon, but he lost all motivation four months into his regimen, stopped eating right and exercising, and never even started the race.

Like Samantha and Brian, you've probably had the experience of working diligently toward an important goal, only to find that you can't reach the finish line. Your goal may be perfectly reasonable and your game plan sound, but somewhere along the line something gets in the way—and it's not a loss of interest. Maybe you stop because you start to second-guess yourself. Perhaps you lose sight of the big picture and forget why you're working so hard. Or you just plain get distracted. Whatever the reason you lose momentum, one thing is sure: no matter how pragmatic your agenda or how serious your intentions, you will lose your way between where you are and where you want to be if you don't nurture your progress every step of the way.

More than just rewarding yourself appropriately with concrete tokens as you make headway with your goals, nurturing your progress involves fortifying yourself emotionally, mentally, and psychologically as you weave through the inevitable obstacles on any road to success. Nurturing your progress means stepping back and seeing yourself from a compassionate, faithful distance so that you can cheer yourself on, boost your confidence, and stoke your passion for your undertaking when the going gets tough. Nurturing your progress means always keeping an optimistic, acclaiming eye on your full potential.

If you've ever taught a child a new skill, supported a good friend through an unbearable breakup, or helped a significant other recover from losing a valued job, then you know how to believe in someone when they don't believe in themselves. That, in essence, is what nurturing progress, coaching really, is all about. You hold someone's desired outcome when he or she doesn't have enough confidence or stamina to embrace what you know they are capable of. The trick to nurturing your own progress is maintaining an objective enough stance as you work toward your goals to coach yourself when necessary. The suggestions below will show you how to keep yourself feeling hopeful and encouraged as the steps toward your goals unfold and your resolve gets tested.

Keep your outcome at the forefront. Many goals get abandoned before completion when we focus on the difficulty of the journey and lose sight of the considerably better-feeling light at the end of the tunnel. Dwelling on the clumsy first few weeks of getting yourself to the gym, watching your spending, or giving up cigarettes will surely depress and deflate you. On the other hand, envisioning how you will feel and what your life will be like when you've gotten in shape, saved a pile of money, or kicked a destructive habit will give you the energy and self-assurance necessary to catapult yourself into lasting behavioral change. The key here is to reduce the discomfort associated with the awkward first steps by envisioning your desired outcome in all its glory. It's similar to imagining your child riding his bike just fine down the street as he wobbles back and forth and falls over and over again while he learns the art of balance. Holding your own outcome in mind gives you patience and perseverance as you push through the graceless beginning of learning something new.

Take fear and doubt along for the ride. Another big reason why people don't bring their well-laid plans to fruition is that they regard anxiety, uncertainty, and other unsettling emotions and associated disconcerting thoughts as signals that they don't have what it takes to be successful. No matter how much experience we have with learning and changing, we forget that the transition from one stage to another almost always makes us hesitant and wary. Because our brains and nervous systems thrive on the predictability and consistency of routine, even when we're downright bored with it, most of us experience new undertakings as unnerving at various points along the way. Whether you're looking to move to a different neighborhood, read your poetry out loud at a poetry slam, or be more assertive at the office, you may feel scared and suddenly lose confidence once the initial excitement of committing to your new goal has given way to the personal risks involved.

What's important to remember here is that courage means going forward *despite* fear and doubt, not without them. You would encourage a friend to keep a big job interview regardless of her last minute jitters because you know she will get to the other side of her panic and quite likely land this job for which she is perfectly qualified. Likewise, it's important to nudge yourself when your own fears and doubts flare up. During moments of uncertainty, you can bring yourself back to a place of reason by focusing on how much better you will feel when you achieve your desired outcome. Instead of fighting your fear and doubt, which is usually a losing, not to mention exhausting, battle, imagine the considerably more pleasant feelings you will experience when you hear the applause after you read your first poem, host your first dinner party in your new neighborhood, or see your colleagues respect you more after you've stood up for yourself at work. The more you let your desired outcome stimulate your emotions, the less effective your fear and doubt will be at stalling your progress.

Speak nicely to yourself. Another obstacle that prevents goal accomplishment is unconstructive self-talk, which amounts to saying discouraging, undermining, and punitive things to yourself as you take a step forward or experience a setback. For some reason, and I don't know why this is, adults feel much more comfortable talking to themselves negatively than positively, and this tendency often comes out full force in the throes of personal realization. It is so much easier when we are feeling challenged to say to ourselves, "I'll never get through this" or "I'm not good enough to make the grade" than it is to say, "I'll survive this somehow" or "I'm just as qualified as anyone else." We all know how vital the soothing words of others are when we're feeling down and out, and yet we don't do very well at offering this kind of encouragement to ourselves when we need extra reinforcement. To figure out what to say to yourself when you need a lift, think about what you'd say to that kid learning to ride a bike when he falls off, starts to cry, and tells you that he can't do it. You don't respond by saying, "You're right. You're uncoordinated and stupid and you might as well give up." That vision of him eventually riding his bike with abandon, maybe even with no hands, is so clear and sharp you can taste it, and you say with absolute and unwavering conviction, "This is hard and learning takes time. You're doing a really great job, and I'm so proud of you. I know you're going to get it soon, so let's keep trying."

The most powerful way of talking to yourself is to keep your focus on your desired outcome by speaking to yourself as if you *already are* where you want to be. So, if you're in the process of decluttering your house, you might say to yourself, "I feel free and light in my spacious, uncluttered house." If you're working at becoming a better money manager, you might say, "I feel more financially organized and secure." If you're learning to keep your life more balanced, you could say, "I feel calm and centered from putting my health first at home and work." Affirming statements like these work best when you speak or write them repeatedly so that your brain can get used to your positive messages. Keep in mind that when your affirming statements are about the feelings you will experience when your desired outcome is achieved, you activate the empowering emotions needed to disarm your negative thoughts. The most important thing to remember about speaking nicely to yourself is that your affirming statements should be reasonable or your brain will reject them. In other words, if you're just starting to exercise, you'll want to say to yourself, "I feel more confident and clear-headed from being more physically active" rather than, "I feel on top of the world from winning my first body-building competition." Once an affirming statement becomes reality, you create a new affirming statement to get you to the next level. When you've gotten used to being more physically active, for example, you can up the ante reasonably by saying to yourself, "I feel focused and fit from exercising regularly and eating nutritiously " and so on.

Take a time out when you need it. Even if you have a beautiful action plan and you're following all the above suggestions, there will be times when you run out of steam as you work toward your goals. If you've been clipping along nicely writing a short story, customizing the internet to your needs, or managing your schedule better, and then for no rational reason can't summon the energy to keep going, a break may be in order. No matter how passionate you are about whatever you're pursuing, you have to get away on occasion to reinvigorate yourself for the journey ahead. If you've watched a loved one beat away relentlessly at a stubborn problem, you know the good that comes from pulling that person away and distracting her with a suitable diversion for a while. So instead of rallying yourself to keep going when you find yourself feeling tired, stuck, or depleted, have lunch with a friend, go out for ice cream, play a game of mini golf, do some yard work, or take a vacation. Some people worry that if they let go and relax before a goal is accomplished, they will never get back on track. But trust me on this: if you're really committed to an agenda, you'll find your way back to it when your energy and enthusiasm are restored. Your intuition will let you know when you're ready.

Apply the Wisdom

- Sit somewhere comfortable and quiet and close your eyes. Envision your ideal outcome of an important goal you're working toward. Imagine what it will be like, feel like, look like when your goal is accomplished. Where are you? What are you wearing? Who is with you? What time of year is it? What do you hear? What does success taste like, feel like, look like, sound like? Call up your outcome from all of your senses to bring it fully into the present. Write down what you imagined and read it out loud to yourself. How do you feel?

- Ask a friend to engage in a conversation with you as if you have both accomplished goals you are currently working on. Speak to each other as if you are in the future, telling each other about your new circumstances. If you are trying to sell your house, you might describe to your friend how great it feels to have money in the bank from the sale of your home and how much you love your new house. If you are working at getting along better with a trying person in your life, you might tell your friend all about your much improved relationship with this person. See how you feel after your conversation.

- Make note of any fears and doubts you have in regard to goals you are working on. Write these fears and doubts down, and pinpoint the ones that seem to get in your way the most. Now ask your intuition what you can do to lessen those annoying feelings and see what you come up with. (And remember to give your intuition ample time and space to process your request and get back to you.)

- Come up with five affirming statements to support yourself as you work on a goal that is particularly exciting to you. Remember to keep your statements in line with your ideal outcome so that you don't reject them. (If you feel overlooked in your job and intend to be taken more seriously, "I feel more confident now that I've asked my boss for a raise" will work way better than "I feel unstoppable now that my salary has tripled.") Train yourself to really believe these statements fully by posting them in prominent places (on your bathroom mirror, refrigerator door, computer screen, or dashboard, for example) and/or writing them 10 times per day for one week. See how you feel at the end of the week, and adjust your affirming statements if necessary to get yourself to the next step.

- Assess your energy level and focus in terms of the goals you are working on. Ask yourself frankly whether you might need a break from one or more of your goals to reignite your commitment. If you need a break, take one. If not, at least come up with some break ideas so that you'll be ready when the time comes.

- If your goals feel unmanageable even after an intermission, consider that you may need to break your steps down further, that you may be working on too many goals simultaneously, or that you may have lost interest in one or some of your goals. Adjust your action plan accordingly.

- If fear and doubts are preventing you from working on your goals, even after you've applied all the suggestions in this chapter, re-read chapter 10 and consider whether an underlying issue may need addressing.

{ chapter 20 }
Have Faith

I am not at all surprised that I live happily in Maine because I knew from an early age that I would settle in New England. Since my childhood visits to my grandparents' home in Massachusetts from Ottawa, Canada, where I grew up, I have always been drawn here. I can't quite put my finger on it, but there's something about the colonial history, the clapboard houses and red brick buildings, the lore of the deep blue sea, the breathtaking mountaintop vistas, the intimate lay of the land that pulls me like a magnet to this part of the country. I have lived in and visited many other wonderful places, but New England is the only spot where I have ever felt completely at home.

Until my 1998 move to Maine from Illinois, where I'd lived since college graduation 13 years earlier, I had always felt like I was on my way somewhere else. No matter how hard I tried to make other places feel right -- Ottawa, then Florida for high school, New Orleans for college, Chicago for my career—so that I wouldn't have to inconveniently uproot myself and start over, my intuition never let up with the clear and consistent message that only New England would ever fulfill me. So convincing was this unrelenting inner message that I gave up a great life in the Windy City – fabulous friends, loving boyfriend, loads of professional contacts—to answer the knock of opportunity in the form of a yearlong doctoral training stint at the University of Maine. All I had to do was get here, my intuition assured me, and my restlessness would cease, my resistance to commitment would stop, and everything would fall into place.

And that's exactly what happened. Even though I didn't know anyone in Maine and missed my Chicago connections fiercely, I immediately knew upon arriving that I was here to stay. As if by magic, my intuition switched its message without hesitation from "You must not settle for anything until you get to New England" to "You're exactly where you belong and now your life can take hold." Despite the uncertainty of adjusting to a new place and despite my initial loneliness, that wondrously affirming new intuitive message was all I needed to believe that my refusal to compromise was about to pay off handsomely—and fast.

So cocky was I from the heady feeling of being instantly gratified for holding out and trusting my intuition all those years, I was convinced that my hard-earned fulfillment in New England would unfurl on precisely my schedule and on my terms. What I wanted most at age 34 was what I'd defied in all those other places I'd lived because I just knew it was waiting for me here where my soul belonged—and that, of course, was my soul mate. My career as a psychologist was beginning to take shape, I was finally where I wanted to be geographically, and so it just made sense that marriage was the next step. After all, hadn't I waited long enough to meet Mr. Right?

For a while, my expectation that marriage was just around the corner made every chance encounter with the opposite sex exhilarating and every blind date an event to look forward to. But soon, as bad dates began to pile up, I started to get angry and frustrated. I kept impatiently wondering what the heck was going on. I had done everything right—listened to my inner voice, stayed true to myself, remained positive in the face of adversity, envisioned a new beginning for myself, persevered toward many valid goals—and I deserved to have this important final piece of my New England picture play out *right now, without further delay*. To my dismay, the more insistent I became, the more losers, and I do mean losers, I attracted: the married man, the untreated alcoholic, the zero emotional intelligence guy, the momma's boy -- and there was even a stalker! Finally, eight years into my otherwise successful New England life as a single woman, I got tired of wishing and hoping for something that might never materialize and threw my hands up for the last time. I'd rather live the rest of my life solo, I decided, than be on the maddening, seemingly futile look-out for Mr. Right any longer. To my amazement, I felt unexpectedly light and liberated when I determined that, married or not, I had a very satisfying life. Never before had I experienced such an energizing, freeing sensation of letting go.

Then, exactly two weeks later, when I least expected it, while having fun with my friends and not even thinking about men, I met Mike, the man who is now my husband.

I tell this personal story to illuminate the most critical part of creating the life you want for yourself, which also happens to be the most challenging part to get down. What I'm speaking of is the capacity to trust that what's genuinely right for you will come to be if you focus on what is within your power and let go of what you have no say in or dominance over. What I'm talking about here is the ability to believe that, no matter how long it takes, how exasperated you become, or how hopeless your situation seems, your efforts will lead to some kind of satisfaction if they are aligned with who you are at your core. Sometimes your payoff will come quickly, sometimes it will take years, sometimes it will come and go and come and go before it stays, and quite often it will come in a wholly unrecognizable form. But it will come, one way or another, if you keep at it.

All you have to do is have faith.

Faith is a complicated matter because it embodies spirituality and religion, which can lead to arguments about whether or not God, Allah, or Something Greater is out there watching over us, protecting us, guiding us, and delivering to us. Most of us think about faith in terms of whether or not we believe in the presence of some higher power that will assist us in achieving our goals if we just accept our mortal limitations and surrender to whatever version of the almighty rings most true for us. From this perspective, those of us who don't believe in a higher power can't have faith and therefore have only luck to depend on if we choose to loosen our grip.

But really, if you think about it, faith has very little to do with whether or not you believe in Something Greater or not. Because, quite frankly, whether you're a devout churchgoer, a diehard atheist, or anyone between these extremes, controlling what you can and letting go of the rest will have the same impact. Whether you believe that letting go will put your problems in the hands of a protective spiritual force or that letting go will simply let you take a break from being constantly in command, you will end up feeling less uptight and more open to opportunity. So if you're convinced that Something Greater exists and that praying to that being will help you along, that's terrific. I say go for it. And if you think that Something Greater is hogwash and religion is a panacea for the gullible, I say why not let go anyway and see what happens? Regardless of your belief system, faith is simply trusting that if you stop trying to control what you can't control and channel your energy into the areas under your rule, things will go more smoothly for you all the way around.

So how do you get to a place where you're doing all you can reasonably do to accomplish something in life, so you can let go and allow things to unfold? How *do you* have faith?

For me, having faith is a practical way to ease angst and sleep better. I am a Unitarian Universalist, meaning that I embrace all forms of spirituality but don't know for certain whether Something Greater is out there. Life is a mystery to me, filled with questions I may never have the ability to answer. Why did my most positive, well-adjusted, accomplished friend get struck down by a fast-moving, fatal neurological disease at age 36 when she was doing everything you're supposed to do to stay healthy? Why is my father, once the most sensible, appreciative person I've very known, bedridden in a nursing home with no quality of life and no end in sight? And why did my mother-in-law, an uncommonly resilient and independent woman who has endured more than her share of hardship, have to lose all her money to the fraudulent financial adviser our whole family trusted? What I know at my age is that peace of mind comes from letting unanswerable questions like these *just be* and focusing instead on doing the best I can with what's certain. Faith is knowing that if I learn what I can from tragedy—that life is precious and short and worth living to the fullest with the strengths I have and the people I love as long as I can— life, even with all its unsolved mysteries, will somehow make some sort of sense in the end.

One great thing about getting older is that we realize from involvement in increasingly complex and dubious situations that black and white, formulaic recipes for success usually don't exist. And from that realization comes a greater ability to accept the limits of our influence. As we evolve, it becomes easier, for example, to see that having the best parents and teachers in the world is no guarantee that a child, ultimately driven by his own individual viewpoint, will make wise choices in life. Or that even if we graduate with honors and enter the workforce with stellar connections, there is no guarantee, in the face of competition and other ever-changing factors in the world of work, that we will achieve our career goals. Again, we can apply our strengths as best we can in line with our truest values, but the only promise we'll ever have is that that we'll grow in some way—if not by reaching our desired objective outcome then by learning something new about ourselves that may help us embrace life more or do better next time.

Having faith requires that you practice the art of getting out of your own way and letting go whenever you can. It's like trusting that if you keep your car in prime condition, honor the speed limit, respect other drivers, and stay alert while you're driving, you will probably make it through the raging snowstorm you have no control over. It's like believing that if you offer great service, treat your clients well, and manage your budget responsibly, your business will be more likely to survive in the tough economy you have no influence on. It's like expecting that if you eat nutritiously, exercise regularly, and surround yourself with supportive people, you will start to feel more steady and balanced in the fast-paced world you can't slow down. Once you see the good that comes from restricting your energy to what you do have authority over, your faith will begin to grow.

The kind of faith that will get you somewhere is not passive or blind. Jumping into a relationship or get rich quick scheme and keeping your eyes closed to red flags is stupidity. Picturing the ideal job and sitting around waiting for the phone to ring is laziness. In other words, real faith is about doing your part—entering a new relationship with a levelheaded amount of caution so you can heed warning signs if there are any, for example, or managing your job search from every angle that's yours to manage—and accepting that the best outcome will manifest when you've done your homework. Faith alone isn't enough. It's a combination of knowing what you want, setting and accomplishing reasonable goals to get there, harnessing hope and confidence, and then allowing room for happenstance, divine intervention, serendipity, and other abstract dynamics to enter in.

The hardest thing about having faith is making space for the unknown in a culture that's all about solid deadlines, obvious solutions, and absolute answers. Because we are told that we can be whoever we want to be, do whatever we want to do, and find whatever answers we want to find, many of us are convinced that if we haven't gotten exactly what we want, it's because we haven't looked hard enough. We have little patience for ambiguity, and so when something doesn't make sense to us right away, we quickly move on in search of instantly evident resolutions. We keep looking for the right partner, house, promotion, diet, whatever result we're after, with the expectation that the outcome will precisely match the picture we've conjured up in our minds, according to the schedule we've imagined. Having faith is realizing that, no matter how prepared or sure you are, what you want often comes to you in its own sweet time, in a way that you can't always anticipate. You may be looking for your life partner in the form of a blue-eyed, college-educated conversationalist and find yourself falling in love with a strong, silent high school drop-out. You may be primed for a new professional opportunity when out of nowhere life throws you a personal problem to grow from. You may be dedicated to saving money for a trip around the world when a medical diagnosis forces you to invest your travel fund in taking better care of yourself.

You can't always direct what happens to you and when, but, if you know what's important to you overall and what you want to get out of life, you can have faith that, even if everything comes out of order and contradicts the particular visuals you have in mind, you will end up at the end of your life with the sense of satisfaction and fulfillment we all seek. If you want faith to work for you, the secret is to move slowly with an open mind so that you see opportunities, however disguised or out of sync with your expectations, as they begin to present themselves. Faith won't prevent aging, loss, death, and other painful experiences all humans endure, and it won't guarantee solutions to all the problems you encounter. What faith will do is free you to drop the burden of pointless worrying and apply yourself to the much more constructive work of conducting yourself to the best of your ability within your jurisdiction.

Apply the Wisdom

- Think of times in your life when a lack of faith has led to poor results. For example, maybe you came across as less competent in a job interview or boring on a date because you were anxious. Consider how greater faith might have led to better results. Now ask yourself how greater faith could put current circumstances more in your favor.

- Get a piece of paper. Create two columns by drawing a horizontal line across the top and a vertical line from top to bottom. At the top of the left column write: *What I will do*. At the top of the right column write: *What my assistant will do*. Now, think of a situation over which you have limited control. In the *"What I will do"* column, list all the things you can do to feel more empowered. In the *"What my assistant will do"* column, list all the things you have no control over and don't want to lose sleep worrying about. The example below shows how you might delegate responsibilities if your son is moving away to start college and you are afraid he won't handle his independence well:

What I Will Do	What My Assistant Will Do
Give my son guidelines for handling an emergency.	Help my son to make smart decisions.
Check in with him by phone and email him twice a week.	Help him make good friends at college so he feels supported away from home.
Let him know I'm here if he needs me.	Keep him safe.
Take him shopping for all the supplies he'll need for his first semester.	Help me not to worry so much.

Here's how you might delegate responsibilities if you're trying to sell your house:

What I Will Do	What My Assistant Will Do
Find a reliable realtor.	Send serious house-hunters my way.
Follow the realtor's suggestions for making my house as appealing as possible to buyers.	Attract the perfect buyer.
Stop listening to negative talk about the housing market.	Help me to tune out unnecessary negativity about the housing market.
Get my family on board with keeping the house clean and free of clutter.	Keep me feeling calm and optimistic through the ups and downs of the sales process.

- Once you've delegated responsibilities accordingly for whatever goal you've chosen to work on, stand back and look at what you've written. Do you feel more focused on what you can control now that you've separated out what is beyond your control and handed it over to your assistant? Now, consider working on your plan of action, and think about your assistant as the entity entrusted with handling whatever unmanageable factors are creating anxiety. Try this technique in any situation that causes you concern and see if it helps you let go and trust that things will be okay if you concentrate on doing your part.

- Having faith is easier when you feel comfortable with uncertainty, mystery, and gray areas. To get away from the American idea that firm deadlines and concrete answers are a given, take a break from American mainstream movies, TV shows, and blockbuster novels that embody our demand for certainty by wrapping everything up nicely by the end. You can strengthen your ability to deal with the unknown, and perhaps even develop a taste for ambiguity, by reading short stories and watching foreign films, many of which mirror life more realistically by leaving things hanging at the end.

- Have there been times in your life when what you got was far from what you expected and you ended up being grateful later? Maybe you found a better apartment after getting turned down for the one you were counting on. Perhaps the job you didn't get led you to a professional opportunity that you never saw coming. Or maybe you couldn't locate that perfect birthday gift you had in mind for a friend and then stumbled upon a gift that turned out to be even more ideal. Have instances when initial disappointment turned into unexpected success down the road helped to strengthen your faith?

- Make a list of various small, inexpensive items you need in your house. For example: pair of pliers, serving platter, throw pillow, soap holder, flower vase, and book ends. Dedicate a weekend morning to shopping at thrift stores, flea markets, and yard sales, with no expectations, your mind open to whatever you might find, and just one rule: you won't blow your money on anything you don't absolutely want and need. What was your experience like? Did you find any unexpected surprises? Was shopping more fun when you didn't feel pressure to find exactly what you put on your list? What did this experience teach you about faith? How might you apply this approach to make other areas of your life easier?

- Ask yourself frankly if there are situations in your life where you've invested too much faith and not enough actual work. Are you really doing all you can do within your power to accomplish your goals? Are you relying too much on Something Greater to carry you through? If you find that you're doing less than your share, pinpoint some small ways that you can step up to the plate more to get the job done.

{ chapter 21 }
Shoot for a Climate of Consistancy

Ray, a 47-year-old entrepreneur, comes to his third therapy session ready to throw in the towel. He reports that his wife, colleagues, and friends have all told him he seems to be making great progress—they've noticed that he's smiling more and is easier to get along with—but he feels more stressed than he has ever felt. "I came to see you because I was depressed, and now I know what a positive attitude can do for me, but it's just too hard to work at it all the time," he explains. "Every minute of the day I'm on myself, telling myself to cheer up and focus on the good so I don't slip back into that awful place. I look fine on the outside, but I'm terrified that I won't be able to keep this up, and I'm totally exhausted from micromanaging every single thought I have."

Valerie, a 41-year-old real estate broker who has just moved across the country with her husband and three kids, comes to see me complaining of understandable anxiety and fatigue. She tells me she has always been an extroverted, upbeat risk-taker, and is feeling uncharacteristically on edge and tired from the stress of uprooting herself and starting a new job. "I've gone through a lot of change in my life and I know I'll adjust eventually," she says. "I'm worried, though, because I've been to a ton of seminars on the power of positive thinking, and lately I just haven't felt very grateful. I'm afraid I'll start pushing everything away if I don't get back to appreciating all the abundance in my life."

Ray and Valerie share a predicament that many enlightened clients bring to me. Once they realize their capacity to enhance their circumstances by optimizing their strengths, operating with optimism, and otherwise focusing on possibility, they assume that success now hinges on thinking and feeling positively *all* of the time. The worry seems to be that their gains from newfound hope, receptivity, and clarity will crumble, leaving them lost and defeated and back at square one if they allow even one shred of fear, one inkling of ingratitude, or one stray doubt to creep into their new and improved consciousness.

The problem with this all-or-nothing viewpoint—I must always feel good and act happy to be successful—is that it creates unreasonable expectations and tremendous pressure that will eventually burn out even the most enthusiastic and ambitious. Yes, it's true that people who take responsibility for their well-being are more likely than others to enjoy success in life. And it's also true that success generally comes from envisioning a desired outcome and walking into it with a spirit of transcendence. But it's more true that a genuinely balanced sense of accomplishment comes from embracing the ups and downs we all encounter as we work toward our goals.

Ask any honest and admirable athlete, executive, artist, actor, or other consummate professional how they've gotten where they are, and they will tell you that they have developed an acceptance of failure as an integral part of success. They will explain to you that their sport, trade, craft, business acumen, whatever talent or skill that sets them a part, is one that they practice. They hone, sharpen, wrestle with, learn from, and become humbled and challenged by it on an ongoing basis.

The central word here is practice.

To become really good at something, no matter what it is you want to be good at, you have to do it over and over, making improvements little by little, until it gets easier overall. No matter how good you get at shooting baskets, handling conflict, sketching portraits, raising kids, seeing the glass as half full instead of half empty, you will have moments, hours, days, sometimes weeks when you're unable to focus, filled with reservations, riddled with insecurity, or just plain off your mark. Sometimes an external interruption, like a family emergency, sudden layoff, or natural disaster, will throw you off course. Other times an inner interruption, like an illness or biological condition, fatigue, or just a plain old bad mood or case of self-doubt will knock you down. The point is that success is more a back-and-forth, up-and-down process than a straight shot. You just do the best you can every day, take the good with the bad, learn from your mistakes, and get back at it tomorrow. Smart people know that perfection is an inspiring ideal, not a plausible destination. And failure, as movie star of the silent screen Mary Pickford so aptly put it, "is not the falling down but the staying down."

What all this means as you move forward with what you've learned from this book is that the climate is more important than the weather. Just as occasional downpours don't make Florida a rainy state, intermittent downbeat notions don't turn an optimist into a pessimist, and sporadic bouts of taking life for granted don't make an appreciative person an ingrate. Likewise, if you make mostly healthful food choices, giving in to an occasional hankering for chocolate isn't going to topple your diet. If you're by and large a reasonable person, being cranky every now and then won't make you emotionally unintelligent. And if as a rule you follow through on what you promise, an infrequent episode of forgetfulness won't brand you unreliable. What counts is what you think, how you behave, how you feel, and who you are *more often than not*.

Our culture is hooked on quick-fix, one-stop promises. Find complete inner peace by attending a one-day seminar, improve your self-esteem once and for all by reading this or that article, get the body you want in three easy payments, just picture what you desire in your mind and it will manifest before you. That's why it's not easy to hear that even if you work really hard at something, you will never get it totally right all of the time. But I'm telling you now that you can expect to fall off the wagon, most likely repeatedly, after you've finished this book. I hope knowing this will help you be kinder to yourself when you're less able to carry out your newfound wisdom. Knowing that your plans to live your life more in accord with the principles I've outlined will definitely be disrupted—either by outside demands or your own shifting mood and energy level -- actually better prepares you for success.

Be forewarned. If you force yourself to stick unremittingly to your new intentions, your motivation will quickly give way to a sense of sheer drudgery. Pushing yourself forward when you simply don't feel like moving or when outside events block you will turn the excitement of your new outlook into a punishing, fatiguing ordeal. By this point you know that charging ahead without checking in with your feelings and doing what you can to honor them is the one sure way to deplete and discourage yourself. So, in the spirit of trusting yourself as you've learned to do when facing the inevitable roadblocks ahead, check in with yourself whenever you lose momentum and ask your intuition for direction.

Ray, my client whose unwavering commitment to thinking positively was making him more stressed, realized upon some introspection that the obsessiveness that had helped him keep his business organized would not work with his personality goals. I convinced him to stick with therapy, and he slowly began to see that thinking positively most of the time rather than every moment of the day was good enough to make his life steadily better. Valerie, my relocated real estate client, soon understood that renewed balance would come from allowing herself to vent her way through her adjustment. As she became increasingly more comfortable with letting go and allowing herself to recover from her move and settle into her new life, she noticed that all she had built did not disappear as she'd feared. To her surprise, she saw that making room for all of her feelings, not just the merry ones, led to a greater capacity for appreciation.

The important thing to keep in mind is that every positive stride you make does count. Anytime you make up your mind to modify your life, to aspire to more productive ways of feeling, thinking, and behaving, you will be faced with undoing ingrained habits that are hard to break. Whether it's sloppiness, workaholism, gossiping, or talking too much that you're trying to eradicate, your brain will fight hard to hold onto automatic habits and avoid the hard work of change. In the same way that getting around town requires more effort when you're in a new place and need a map to navigate, adapting to new styles of working and living demands more focus and energy than usual. That's why, especially in the beginning of any kind of transformation, you will probably revert to your old ways when your stress level increases. Your brain can handle only so much. It's easier to go back to an old habit, like eating or shopping compulsively, to cope rather than continuing your new exercise habit when you have a particularly bad day at the office.

For some irrational reason, all of us discount any progress made at times like this and decide we might as well give up. If we blow our budget or our diet, we figure all is lost so we might as well just go for broke rather than do what's smart: put the brakes on, acknowledge that you've slipped up, call it a day, and resolve to get back on track tomorrow. Sometimes a good night's sleep is really all you need to regroup; other times you may need a longer break. The point is that you will eventually get back to adopting your new norm. The more you practice, the easier it becomes to resume in a more productive direction after the inevitable internal or external curveball arrives. Your thoughts, feelings, and behavior will never be 100 percent pure and flawless. But if you make it your custom to live and work in concert with what intuitively feels healthful and smart to you, falling down and getting back up until your new ways are your norm, it will eventually be your new and improved habits that are hard to break.

Apply the Wisdom

- Choose a habit you want to develop. Maybe you want to eat dessert only on holidays and birthdays, put your clothes away instead of leaving them in a pile on your floor at the end of the day, or drive without talking on your cell phone. Now keep track in a journal or notebook of every time you successfully implement your new behavior. For example, write down every time you refuse dessert, put your clothes away, or resist picking up your cell phone while you're behind the wheel. Look at your list every so often and see how you feel. Does keeping track of your successes help you to see that exceptions do add up to become the rule?

- Think of the accomplishments, skills, and talents you are most proud of. Now look back and consider the ups and downs of what you have created for yourself. Do you have more confidence in your capacity to make lasting change in your life when you revisit the trials and errors behind your triumphs?

- Make a list of the people with whom you are closest— your partner, parents, siblings, children, friends, and colleagues. How would you describe these people in terms of personality? Do any of these people fit the personality label you've given them all of the time? Have any of these people gotten anything right all of the time? See if this exercise helps you take your own imperfections and failures with a grain of salt and focus more on the rule than the exception. (And, by the way, if you do happen to have a close friend, relative or colleague who is perfect all the time, please let me know. I'd really like to meet that person.)

- As you work to instill new norms in your life, come up with some affirming statements you can say to yourself. Here's one I like: "I'm doing the best I can with what I have to make the most of this day."

- Read biographies of people you admire to learn new ways of coping with the ups and downs of success.

{ chapter 22 }
Take the Insights with You

Here you are. You've made your way almost to the end of this book. By now you've considered many new ideas for getting out from under the near-constant call to do it all, have it all, be it all, and are asserting your own rules for success. You've tested some new ideas for feeling more centered and capable and are generally better able to function productively and harmoniously despite the unyielding demands and distractions that have come to define American culture. Hopefully, you are already enjoying positive changes from that experimentation.

Now, as you conclude, you are wondering how, when you close the cover of this book, to incorporate the strategies you've learned and continue to experience the benefits of this book on your own. You don't want this to be just one more self-help book that leaves you feeling temporarily pumped up with impractical promises. What you do want is a viable plan that translates to the challenges you face out in the world. And fortunately, if you've gotten what I've intended to give you, you will not be disappointed.

As you recall from the beginning pages, my agenda here is to provide you with an upgraded framework for realizing your personal and professional goals. The way to feel successful, I advised you initially, is to restructure your foundation for solving problems, making decisions, and otherwise maneuvering toward increasing levels of actualization. The skills you learned in adolescence for considering options, weighing consequences, and committing to various personal and professional paths, I explained, no longer work so effectively because they have become outdated. For those of us who mastered the art of achievement in an era when there was far more constancy and considerably less choice, retraining is required to get us up to speed with a markedly more hurried and diversified context for growth and development.

What thriving comes down to in this frenzied day and age is adopting a perspective that embodies the qualities required to stay sturdy and steady amid the ever-maddening commotion:

- Discernment to separate the essential from the superfluous.

- Self-awareness to know what you can and can't handle, and what you do or don't need or want.

- Resilience to weather the ceaseless barrage of change and transition.

- Foresight to look beyond enticing social standards and imagine your own goals and dreams.

- Patience to get along with yourself and others in stressful situations.

- Determination to stay the course despite disruption.

- Pragmatism to know when enough is enough.

- Humility and humor to not take the call to do it all, have it all, and be it all so darned seriously.

Cultivating these qualities inherent in the calm-amid-the-storm approach I'm advocating is difficult, deliberate work. But investing your resolve in the effort will allow you to step away from the cacophony, see the big picture, ground yourself, zero in on options that are most resonant for you, and make informed, insightful decisions about where and how you want to grow and evolve.

You know by now that peace of mind, greater confidence, fulfillment, security, and purpose—the hallmarks of adult satisfaction most of us are looking for from our personal and professional improvement endeavors—can't be arrived at in quick-fix, one-stop-shopping fashion. The good news is that these sought-after hallmarks are obtainable byproducts of living according to the principles outlined in this book. As I've said a number of times, there is no way to avoid the inevitable struggles of being human or reverse the ever-escalating pace of American life. But you will be less susceptible to the overwhelm and more hardy in the face of inexorable adversity if you resist seductive yet superficial solutions and get on with building a deeper and more lasting reserve of wisdom and tenacity with which to steer yourself. Your blueprint for living life on your terms—no matter the whirlwind surrounding you—is encompassed in these ten not-so-easy but simple and straightforward steps:

Deal with reality. If you want to succeed in a culture that demands your attention at every turn, you can't waste time and energy on denying, escaping, or minimizing inconvenient truths or getting lost in wishful thinking. Your energy is better spent seeing things squarely in the present so that you can figure out how to make the most of your situation. So face the facts. Our culture is not going to slow down. There will always be strife and stress to contend with. You will experience loss, disappointment, failure, illness, and accidents in your life. You will never be perfect. You will never get it all done. You will, if you're lucky, grow old. You will die. There are no guarantees. Weight reduction is best accomplished by eating less and moving more. Your brain will never be capable of focusing simultaneously on two tasks requiring your full concentration. The pay-off from facing reality is that when you stop running from the truth, you automatically become less susceptible to even the most cleverly disguised snake oil, and you are more likely to see real possibility in front of you.

Take excellent care of yourself. Steering yourself where you want to go—and not where advertisers and marketers are trying to push and pull you—requires rock solid verve and stamina. You need to be genuinely rested and awake with all your parts in good working order to cut through the chaos of modern life and see your way to what's important. This means making sure that you get enough sleep, eat reasonably well, exercise sufficiently, protect yourself from people and environments that sap you, keep your brain and heart adequately stimulated, break away from work whenever necessary to take the edge off, have fun and recharge yourself, and get support when you need it. The advantage of taking full responsibility for your physical and mental health is that you'll be well-anchored with your wits about you when the going gets tough.

Galvanize your resources. One sure way you can winnow down the myriad options vying for your attention is to identify your most valuable resources and then channel them into solutions. This means recognizing and fortifying the strengths in yourself, other people, your environment, and the internet and technology. You can't afford to waste time complaining about what's not working, attempting to excel in areas that just aren't your bailiwick, or persuading others to go against their grain. If you find ways to combine your resources to accomplish your goals, you will experience a more streamlined sense of cooperation, collaboration, and competency.

Keep your values at the forefront. You can't get where you want to go unless you know where you're headed. So you need to keep your end point in mind at all times. This means letting what's most important to you—your health, your family and friends, your livelihood, and other core sources of meaning and purpose—inform your decisions. This also means envisioning what you want today – more money in the bank, less weight around your middle, happier relationships at home and the office—so that a clear picture can remind you why you're working so hard and coax you toward fruition. By placing emphasis on your desired outcome, you will be better able to outwit your fears and doubts. And you will be less tempted to take supposed easier routes that ultimately make life harder by compromising what you hold dear.

Dump the extraneous. It's hard to get anywhere in life when you can't see the path in front of you. You can clear your way by ridding yourself of stuff, ideas, goals, commitments, relationships, and obligations that have long since served a purpose and are now only taking up premium space. Identifying and then getting rid of whatever is weighing on you, cluttering your environment, clogging your mind, or dragging you down will free up room for more resonant beliefs, belongings, and opportunities, and you will feel more energized and better able to breathe.

Engage and encourage yourself and others. To stay committed to pursuits that are important to you, you need to shape your progress along the way. This means breaking your goals down and rewarding yourself upon completion of each workable step. Motivating yourself also involves speaking kindly to yourself as you endure the challenge of actualizing your ambitions. And since success can't happen in isolation, your progress in life also requires that you put yourself in the shoes of others so that you can inspire them toward a shared vision in ways that are stimulating and meaningful. If you keep track of your successes and celebrate your accomplishments and do the same for others, you can count on camaraderie to urge you along when you can't see light at the end of the tunnel.

Set and maintain appropriate limits. In a culture that tells us the sky's the limit no matter what our circumstances, you will quickly burn yourself out if you don't know and respect your personal thresholds. You are most apt to be successful when you push yourself enough to exercise your strengths, but not so far out of your league that you're floundering. So make sure not to work, eat, shop, stay awake, lift weights, absorb information, research, perfect yourself, or do anything else beyond what is reasonable. Control what you can control, and let go of the rest. Stop trying to manage time and strive instead to manage yourself within time. Don't try to do too much at once. Know your risk tolerance. Be honest about how much you really need to learn and grow to be happy. And set appropriate social boundaries so that other people enliven rather than deplete you. Healthy limits will structure your progress in a way that rings true for you.

Think through your decisions. When compelling choices are thrust at you 24 hours a day, the natural tendency is to simplify decision making by reacting hastily—and quite often ruefully. You know that only so many choices are right for you, so you must put the brakes on in the face of rapid fire options and take time to respond responsibly. Put a hold on whatever you're craving. Get a handle on intense emotions and impulses before you act on them. Reflect on alternatives and pose the right questions before making your selection. Ask yourself what you really want and need. Look behind the claims of advertising. Lift the curtain of too-good-to-be-true stories. Consider how your actions and behavior will impact others. By taking the necessary time to consider consequences and arrive at responses that feel right, you will experience less regret and more reward—and you will have a reservoir of established self-discipline to keep you on course.

Honor your emotions. Feeling good is the ultimate goal for most of us, the payoff for working so hard and putting up with so much. The cultural message is that if we speed through unpleasant feelings like sadness, disappointment, confusion, anger, and doubt, we will land at our feeling good destination without unnecessary delay. Of course, the reality is that emotional distress is part of every life journey, and ignoring, repressing, and avoiding that distress only makes it try harder to get your attention. It's not healthy to wallow in negative emotions or take your distress out on others, but the only way to get to the other side of the pain is to work through it. So give yourself time to heal and recover when necessary, find healthy outlets for pent up feelings, balance your discomfort with intervals of nourishing escapism, and communicate your feelings respectfully. You can't appreciate victory without knowing adversity, and you will only see the light when you have seen the darkness.

Make room for intuition, Something Greater, and all that is unseen. American life is all about moving quickly to produce what can be undeniably observed, measured, and stamped with a price tag. We have very little patience for or faith in elements that aren't material and visible to the eye, and it is subsequently difficult for us to believe in the power of ambiguous, invisible forces. But if you want to succeed in life, you must rely on your intuition as your most reliable guide, and you must let go of what you can't control and trust that things will somehow work out. Creating the time and space to hear your inner voice will help you to screen out distracting advice and trust your own wisdom. Learning to let go and allow chance and circumstance to intervene in your plans will help you to trust that life, however unpredictable, usually works out better when you apply your own wisdom and then get out of the way.

{ chapter 23 }
Keep Yourself in Check

Practice. There's that word again, and you know where I'm going with this. Reading is not enough. If you want to achieve consistency with the ten principles outlined in the previous chapter, you need to practice them regularly. You know by now that mastery requires that you do something over and over again until you get comfortable enough with it to get it right *most of the time.* It's worth repeating once more that you will never, ever be perfect. You will, however, be more content if you make it a priority to deliberately live your life according to what's been laid out in this book. Your investment in adopting a new and better blueprint will take time and energy, especially in the beginning as you get used to new ways of thinking, feeling, and acting. But the more you go at it, the more natural it will feel. Then you will really have it made.

Great things will happen when you make these principles your starting point for all that you do. By turning away from constantly shifting, whirling, and multiplying outside directives that only make you feel small and stressed, you will gain an automatic sense of focus and direction. As you adhere instead to the ten principles as your primary frame of reference, life becomes a considerably more simple and satisfying process of taking your lead from stalwart and sustaining rules. Because these rules are clear, candid, and specifically designed to bring out the attributes and assets that make you unique, you will feel increasingly powerful and grounded as you employ them.

The secret to making this new blueprint work for you is to apply it as best you can day by day, assessing your performance regularly to gauge your progress. You've learned the importance of making affirming statements to yourself as you work toward your goals—"I am living in line with the blueprint" is much more empowering than "I hope to live in line with the blueprint"—so it makes sense to assume the principles by voicing them in the present tense. You've also learned the importance of reviewing your performance so that you can make necessary refinements. Don't overanalyze. Just assess yourself daily on how much you applied each principle, and use your appraisal to inform your strategy for tomorrow. You will soon see that this blueprint for success has become a constant, central anchor that you will always be able to count on to keep you grounded. No matter how busy or unhinged the world becomes, no matter how many detours you take, no matter how many times you fall down and get back up, you will never lose your way.

Now, here are some practical tips for making the blueprint yours:

Score yourself at the end of each day on how much you applied each principle, with one on the scale being "none of the time" and ten on the scale being "all of the time." Average your scores at the end of the week for a quick overview of what's going best and what needs your attention. And remember: this is not a test. The idea is not to get perfect scores, but to assess yourself day to day and stay accountable with integrating the basics of this book into your life. If you're doing great on some, not so great on others, and averaging 7 or 8 overall, you're doing really well. Try this approach for several weeks and watch your new habits begin to click in.

Base your goals on where your scores are consistently falling low. The areas you're high in probably don't require much refinement. For example, if you can honestly say that you're setting limits well in a particular area of your life, you've probably developed good habits in that area that are already working for you. On the other hand, if you've developed a bad habit of spending too much time at your computer or you're having trouble saying no when people ask you for favors, you'll probably want to pay attention to this area.

Focus on one problem area at a time. Let's say you're overextended at work, not taking very good care of yourself, and your house is filled with junk. If you try to tackle all of these areas of your life at once, you will only become more stressed. If you select just one area, however, and go at it one small, reasonable step at a time, you will likely see real improvement. And the added benefit is that success in one area almost always transfers to other areas. My client Martha, overwhelmed across the map, decided to start with getting her house in order, trusting that she'd have the energy and inspiration to get to other vital areas of her life once she'd unburdened herself of all the physical clutter surrounding her. And you know what happened? Cleaning up her house triggered a domino effect that led to an improved mood, better sleep, a new romantic relationship, and a raise at work.

Allow for fluctuation. Just as your body weight goes up and down on the scale according to vacillating biological circumstances, your scores will change according to what is going on inside and around you. If it's your busy season at work, if your child is ill, if you are planning your wedding, if you're just not in a very good mood, for instance, you may be more overwhelmed than usual and your scores will reflect that. Remember that in these fast-paced times, no plan is ever written in stone. If your scores bend and flex a little, that means you're actively responding to life—and that's the whole point. If your scores are vacillating too widely and you can't think of any obvious reason why, it may be that the goals you're working on within those areas are too lofty or no longer enticing to you. Review your goals routinely to make sure they are not only reasonable, but also still in line with who you are and what you want.

Chart Your Way to Success

Guiding Principles	M	T	W	T	F	S	S	Weekly Average
I deal with reality.								
I take excellent care of myself.								
I make the most of my resources.								
My values are at the forefront.								
I am free of the extraneous.								
I engage and encourage myself and others.								
I set and maintain healthy limits.								
I think through my decisions.								
I honor my emotions.								
I make room for my intuition, Something Greater, and all that is unseen.								

Legend:

1	2	3	4	5	6	7	8	9	10
Least Successful						Most Successful			

(This chart can be downloaded from my web site at amywoodpsyd.com)

{ chapter 24 }
Start Where You Are

I've always known I would write a book. I never had an exact time in mind about when I'd begin to write, but I trusted that my intuition would tell me when I was ready. What ready meant was feeling wise and independent enough to have something worthwhile and distinct to say. Ready also meant feeling truly inspired to write, sensing the words would come naturally, not having to force anything. As I accumulated knowledge and maturity through my personal and professional experiences, my vision of the book began to take shape. My ideas formed gradually over several years, the picture in my mind evolving from book to self-help book to very specific self-help book as those ideas came together.

By the summer of 2009, I was imagining my book so vividly that I knew the time to begin writing was near and I should prime myself. So I recruited a rock-solid, hard-boiled editor. I contemplated how I'd carve out regular writing sessions. I drew up a basic outline. Then, out of the blue, the signal came. I'd just given a talk one weekend in August on how to be successful in life, when a woman approached me enthusiastically. "I think you have a best seller on your hands," she said, as she handed me the business card of her book-publisher husband and urged me to contact him. After a phone meeting a few days later, I had a verbal agreement with the owner of a publishing company in upstate New York that he'd publish my book and I'd have the manuscript to him by spring.   Of course I knew as a well-versed adult that a verbal promise is virtually meaningless in the business world where decisions can change like the wind, but I decided to act as if this publisher's commitment were written in stone because I knew that doing so would propel me nicely toward my deadline. This guy could easily bail on me in the end, but having faith in him would help me to write a quality book that would get published one way or another. Now there was no question that the time had come to get started. And I was all set to go.

One could certainly argue, however, that I really wasn't ready to start my book when I did. Not having a signed publishing contract was just one major reason I wasn't sufficiently prepared, and there were plenty more. Contrary to the advice in two books I'd recently read on how to get a non-fiction book published, I hadn't created an exhaustive proposal to convince prospective agents and publishers that my book would sell in a crowded marketplace. I wasn't a household name, so I couldn't boast an adoring platform of fans I could count on to buy my book. My degrees are far from Ivy League and not in English or journalism, and I've never participated in a non-fiction writing workshop. Plus, I've never had anything published nationally—unless you count the stuffy professional articles that nobody reads. If I'd listened to any expert, who surely would have told me I was foolish to forge ahead without a firm contract and my time and energy would be better spent sharpening my writing skills and finding a well-connected agent, only two things would be certain. You wouldn't be reading this right now. And my intuition would be nagging me incessantly to stop waiting for the time to be any more right and, as Nike says better than anyone, *just do it.*

All I had to go on when I decided to go against rational thought and get started was a history of success doing just that. Because my intuition has always been my guide, I can recount multiple incidents in my life where I have followed my inner voice despite very convincing contrary directions from highly respected sources. My New Orleans college professors warning me not to go to Chicago alone to launch an advertising career because I'd get swallowed up in a big scary city. (I went anyway and landed a job within two weeks.) My graduate school adviser telling me I might as well throw my top three clinical internship applications in the garbage because I'd never even get interviews for such plum programs. (I mailed the applications regardless and got my first choice.)   My post-doctorate fellowship supervisor cautioning me to keep my job with him because I'd never survive the financially uncertain world of self-employment. (My private practice built up to a nice momentum within a year.) My well-meaning friends urging me not to assume the cumbersome baggage of a newly divorced man with two children. (You know how that all turned out.) Experience has shown me again and again that smart risks—risks dictated primarily by gut, that is—usually pay off. That's why I trusted my inexplicable sense that I was prepared enough to write my book.

The point here is that there is rarely a perfect time to begin something important. Especially in a culture that tells us, even when we've reasonably groomed ourselves to launch whatever that important venture is, there is always one more thing to buy, learn, do, become before we are *really* ready. Whether you want to kick a deadbeat spouse to the curb, give up alcohol, can your own vegetables, quit a soulless job, hike the Appalachian Trail, clean out the basement, lose that last five pounds, start a movement, be more social, make a difficult apology, or, yes, put pen to paper and see what happens, there will always be a better time in the future to put your plan into action. When the children leave home, when the holidays are over, when you've taken one more course, when you've gotten one more professional opinion, when you have the right furniture in the living room, when you feel more capable. The problem with this kind of thinking is that if you wait for everything to fall perfectly into place before you take that first step, you will never go anywhere. That's why I say that if your intuition is telling you strongly to do something, you're probably as ready as you're going to be. An inner sense that you're moving in the right direction is the biggest guarantee you'll ever get that your intentions will be realized.

One caveat worth mentioning here is just because your ever-reliable intuition has told you to do something doesn't mean the process will be smooth sailing. Far from it, in fact. If there's one thing I want you to take away from this book, it's that ups and downs are part of life, even when you are taking all the right chances and following your inner voice verbatim. Acting on your intuition won't excuse you from making mistakes, suffering losses, doubting yourself, getting frustrated, becoming distracted, and otherwise experiencing the trials and errors inherent in any worthwhile endeavor. What you can count on, though, is that your intuition will mentor you through those times if you keep yourself open to its subtle cues and prompts. The reassurance that comes from heeding your intuition, even when you're having a major crisis of faith, will eventually get you back in sync.

Even though I knew from the moment I began this book that it was intuitively the right thing for me to do and even though I firmly believed from the start that I could produce a worthy book if I set my mind to it, I got sidetracked many times during the process. Despite the fact that I was channeling my three top strengths—self-discipline, organization, and communication—into a book that embraces my professional specialty, my endeavor was still a major challenge. Even if you set yourself up exquisitely to succeed as I did by using well-honed talents and skills, and even if you are fortunate as I am to have a wonderfully supportive network of family and friends and have to answer only to yourself as a self-employed person, reaching that finish line can be a long, humbling haul.

Over the ten months it took to write this book—and I am referring here to the actual sitting at my laptop and typing part, not the 20-odd prerequisite years of developing the necessary knowledge base for that writing—I generally wrote two days a week with the goal of writing a chapter a week. But that schedule for a variety of reasons didn't always happen. Despite my assuredness, careful planning, and serious dedication, it took a few writing sessions to stare down the blank computer screen, cut through the anxiety that always rears up when I start a daunting project, and start typing. My private practice got too busy and swallowed up my writing time some weeks. Unexpected visitors came to town and seduced me away from my laptop. Internet surfing and emailing occasionally ate up large chunks of writing sessions. A bad head cold came on, and I couldn't muster the energy to write.

Despite my overall confidence and impressive repertoire of motivational skills, undermining fears and doubts occasionally surfaced: "You don't have what it takes to finish this." "You're just one of millions of people trying to get published, so stop kidding yourself." "If you focus too much on writing, you're going to miss out on some very important opportunities." "You're not nearly prepared to do this." "You should get out of your fantasy world and do some work that you know will pay the bills." There were also times when I wanted to write but unanticipated personal events took precedence: helping my sister-in-law Suzie pack for her move into a new apartment, visiting my father after a health scare, attending my niece Sadie's second birthday party, paying last respects to my suddenly dying cousin Ginger. Sometimes my writing didn't happen because I just wasn't in the right frame of mind on the right day. Maybe I'd had one glass of wine too many the night before. My energy or mood was low for some reason. I just hadn't quite worked out how I wanted to approach the chapter in front of me.

Rather than worry each time my momentum got disrupted that I'd never get back to my book, I decided it would be easier to regard unexpected interruptions as essential parts of the writing process. I made the decision at the outset that because this project was intuition inspired, I'd be better off not trying to control it. I'd just trust that any obstacles would resolve themselves if I took charge of what I felt capable of day to day. Because my intuition had commissioned this project, I knew I could count on it to get me through. And so I listened intently to every inner message I heard. *The book will still be here, but Sadie will turn two only once. Beating yourself up isn't going to get you through this stint of writer's block, but taking a walk on the beach or watching a funny movie might do the trick. You won't stand a chance if you get intimidated by the competition and throw in the towel, but you will have a real shot at getting published if you keep at it. Go drink some water, walk the dogs, take a nap with the cats, have some fun, get out of my way for a while, and I'll let you know when I have something for you. Just do your best to complete your weekly chapters, and I'll take care of the rest. Stick with me and your book will materialize.*

Following the advice of my intuition throughout the process of writing this book led to restorative consequences every time. Breaking away when I felt unable to focus always helped me clear my head and make room for the ideas needed to take the book further. And those ideas were often prompted by things I heard, felt, saw, or dreamed up when I was doing something other than writing on my official writing days. Whenever I resumed my writing after those spontaneous sabbaticals, my enlightened viewpoint would make the work of writing more enjoyable and my production more on the mark.

As is always the way, seemingly off-course intuitive instructions usually get you results you couldn't have realized on your own. Had I ignored my inner voice and kept my nose to the grindstone at all costs, pushing through bad moods and illness, pulling all nighters, and skipping meaningful personal events, I probably could have had this book completed by my ideal March 31st deadline as originally intended. Taking all those intuitively mandated breaks postponed my completion date by ten weeks, but the book is far richer from the delays.

By going at this book my way, starting when I felt ready to start rather than waiting for some elusive outside force to deem me ready, pacing myself in accordance with my own rhythms, and enlisting unseen forces to coach me along, I have accomplished something that makes me feel more in tune with myself and the world around me. I'm satisfied because I have completed a self-imposed rite of passage and grown from it, excited about taking a much deserved long summer break, and looking forward to hearing what my intuition has in store for me next. In the end, this full-bodied sense of achievement is far more significant to me than whatever monetary gain or notoriety might come from the product of my passion.

In short, that's what success is all about. It's the unbeatable internal reward you get when you believe in yourself enough to give your innermost hunches a real shot. And it all begins with asking yourself what that one thing is you can do to be more fully yourself. So whatever that one thing is right now, whatever you want to do deep down at this moment, wherever you happen to be, shake off whatever is distracting you, imagine your outcome, and go for it. There really is no time like the present to take your first small step.

{ acknowledgements }

Writing this book was an all-encompassing endeavor involving multiple people – not just those who helped me with the project at hand, but countless friends, relatives, colleagues, supervisors, teachers, and clients who have shaped the lifetime of ideas and inspiration that went into my writing. To thank everyone whose presence I felt as I put words to paper would be a book in itself, so I'll stick to those who were directly influential to me during the year I brought *Life Your Way* into being.

I am indebted to Anne Collins Milford, Rick Dacri, Peter Wood, Susanna Liller, Jack Kahn, and Jim Bouchard for showing me through the publication of their own fine writing that my book was possible.

Immense gratitude goes to Paula Keeney, my incredibly talented editor, who made my words sound more like me and kept me focused and grounded week by week, chapter by chapter.

For taking the time to read my work and offer candid feedback, I am grateful to Mary Preuss Olson, David Wood, Betsy and John Preuss, Mary Coughlan, Jim Bouchard, Diane Freed, Susanna Liller, Jennifer Comeau, Suzie Coughlan, Edite Kroll, Julia Kirby, Jack Kahn, Bob Powers, George Vaillant, Jeffrey Auerbach, Stephanie Limmer, Jeanne Whynot-Vickers, Jeff Fisher, Barbara Babkirk, Anne Collins Milford, and Barbara Wilson.

For helping me to negotiate the ins and outs of the publishing world, appreciation goes to Rick Dacri, Jim Bouchard, Tam Veilleux, Steff Deschenes, and Susan deGrandpre. And much thanks to Beth Harris-Hess and Dan Yeager for their eye-catching design.

As with any major project, there were moments in the writing and publishing process when I lost sight of the light at the end of the tunnel. I thank my dear friend Hideko Sera and her family for so courageously showing what determination, resilience, and faith can do in the face of hardship.

For collectively teaching me how to simultaneously be pragmatic and follow my dreams, I will forever be grateful to the most important role models of my life: my parents, Jane and Richard Wood, and my grandparents, Marian and Ralph Wood.

For making my home the harmonious haven that makes writing a book possible, I thank my endlessly steady, supportive, and sensible husband Mike, my awesome stepchildren Hunter and Ryan, and our wonderful animals Shasta, Morgan, Nickolai, and Honus.

{ about the author }

Amy Wood, Psy.D., a psychologist, helps people to become happier at home and work through writing, speaking engagements, consulting, workshops, and one-on-one sessions. She earned her doctorate at the Adler School of Professional Psychology and is certified by the College of Executive Coaching. She lives in Kennebunk, Maine with her husband, two stepchildren, two dogs, and two cats.   Visit the author online at www.amywoodpsyd.com.

LaVergne, TN USA
09 March 2011
219466LV00001B/194/P